Velocity Revisited

A Quantized Origin for Waves and Relativity

Velocity Revisited

A Quantized Origin for Waves and Relativity

Irwin Wunderman, PhD

This theory endeavors to advance aspirations of Pythagoras and speculations of Dirac.
"There is thus a possibility that the ancient dreams of philosophers to connect all Nature with the properties of whole numbers will someday be realized."
P. A. M. Dirac

authorHOUSE®

AuthorHouse™
1663 Liberty Drive
Bloomington, IN 47403
www.authorhouse.com
Phone: 1-800-839-8640

First published by AuthorHouse   01/18/2012

ISBN: 978-1-4634-3790-9 (sc)
ISBN: 978-1-4634-3791-6 (ebk)

Table of Contents

SECTION I
THE RELEVANT ISSUES

SECTION II

Prologue

Irwin Wunderman, my dad, defied convention, thought freely, and drew his own conclusions. My dad used to tell me that very few people would be able to understand his 'theory of the universe,' our familial metaphor for his ideas on wave propagation, uncertainty, and related topics that have emerged as the major barrier to prediction and scientific certainty. Where does uncertainty come from? Dad would point to ideas like those presented in this book. He always said the answer was elegant and so obvious in his mind. I know I have only a superficial understanding of what he believed to be a significant contribution to the fields of math and science. I hope that whoever is reading this continues to disseminate his ideas.

My father completed "Velocity Revisited" on July 22, 2005. He wanted one of his favorite poems, "Invictus" by Ernest Henley (1849-1903), as the prologue to this book along with two new stanzas that he added at the end. He then re-titled the poem, "Invictus Concluded." My dad passed away unexpectedly of a heart attack the next day.

"Velocity Revisited" is my dad's third book on his theory of the universe. He worked tirelessly on these concepts and formulations for over forty years. I have done my best to edit and determine the sequencing of my father's manuscript. As you will see, there are a few instances where I was not sure of my father's intent regarding placement of his ideas. I have made note of this in the book. I want to thank Andrei Lessiv, PhD, Mario Rabinowitz, PhD and Richard Wunderman, PhD for helping me with the editing, and Allen Amaro for his work with the figures. I regret that it has taken me six years to publish his final work. However, I know that dad can now rest in peace.

Lorna Wunderman Monroe
December 23, 2011

Invictus "Concluded"

William Ernest Henley 1849-1903[1] (all but last two stanzas)

Out of the night that covers me,
Black as the Pit from pole to pole,
I thank whatever the gods may be
For my unconquerable soul.

In the fell clutch of circumstance
I have not winced nor cried aloud.
Under the bludgeoning of chance
My head is bloody, but unbowed.

Beyond this place of wrath and tears
Looms but the Horror of the shade,
And yet the menace of the years
Finds, and shall find, me unafraid.

It matter not how strait the gate,
How charged with punishments the scroll,
I am the master of my fate:
I am the captain of my soul.

When my time comes to leave this place
I shall have savored all that passed,
And when they put me in the grave,
That final move shall be my last.

The earth will spin and orb the sun
As stars intermingle in the sky
My life's work shall be done:
With those thoughts, I say goodbye.

---

[1] (Henley, 1891)

1) Abstract

This book is an elaboration and expansion of work presented in "What is a Photon?"[2] (Wunderman, 2000) and "Planck's Constant and Pi"[3] (Wunderman, 2004) which introduced a new interpretation for the space between integers of the natural number counting system. Mechanisms of wave propagation provide the essence of this theory. In addition, foundations emerge from the natural numbers themselves. The thesis makes a distinction between indeterminism and lack of causality in *de facto* physical processes. This work utilizes an uncommon method to describe how a wave-front surface area grows. The theory can infer a slightly altered interpretation of how space progresses as a square law when advancing away from an origin.

Section I and Section II present an overview of the analysis method. The analysis in this treatise derives circumstances for viably transmitted cyclic modes and the consequence of their existence. Section I addresses the motion of objects like spontaneous emission photons that propagate at the highest rate, light-speed C. **Lowercase c is the traditional symbol for light speed, but because of the importance of the velocity of light, it will be designated as capital C throughout this book.** Section II covers the relative motion of slower rest mass objects. This treatise does not analyze relative motion in the presence of fields like gravity that could act on the moving object. This thesis purports that our interpretation of relative motion, what we call inertial velocity, is best expressed quite differently than has traditionally been done. This thesis hopes to show that the speed of light should numerically be absolute unity, based exclusively on the mechanism by which area accrues on the information-transferring-wave-front generated by events on a moving object. This thesis hopes to demonstrate that a more general type wave description better satisfies portrayal of a photon's "frequency". The harmonic exponential function "e" is therefore purported to be an inappropriate mathematical function for physically representing propagating waves, photon frequencies, electromagnetic-radiation, and affiliated cyclic phenomena. An appropriate function must involve a reaction that temporally follows an initiating cause and presents a response that includes effects of Planck's constant and indeterminism associated therewith. This theory presents such a function and the waves generated are called unified waves.

---

[2]   I. Wunderman (2000). *What is a Photon: A Unified Wave Theory Explained.* Bristol, Indiana: Wyndham Hall Press.

[3]   I. Wunderman (2004). *Plank's Constant and Pi: A Unified Wave Theory for Particles and Bioforms.* Bloomington, Indiana: 1st Books Library.

2) Background

The square root of any two consecutive natural numbers as $\sqrt{[n+(n+1)]} = \sqrt{(2n+1)}$ will only be an integer for the sequence of odd numbers 1, 3, 5, 7, 9, 11,—etc., to ∞. This is also true for the orthogonal vector between radial n-vector and radial vector (n+1) as $\sqrt{[(n+1)^2-n^2]} = \sqrt{(2n+1)}$ as shown in figure 1.

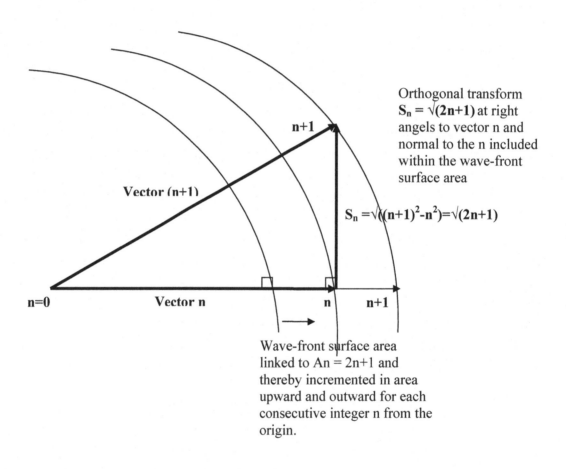

Figure 1 Orthogonal vector between radial vector-n and radial vector (n+1) as $\sqrt{(2n+1)}$

In square law space, this consequential uniform spacing between odd numbers resulting from a square root, affords natural periodicities in sequentially-placed area-increments within a wave-front. An object moving relative to an observer at, or close to, light-speed C emanates a wave-front of its event information that can thereby contain **spatial-periodicities** in the sequence that the wave-front area-increments accrued. As shown in figure 2, these spatial periodicities, as circulatory excursions around the Y and Z directions derive from the temporal frequency that would propagate along direction-X.

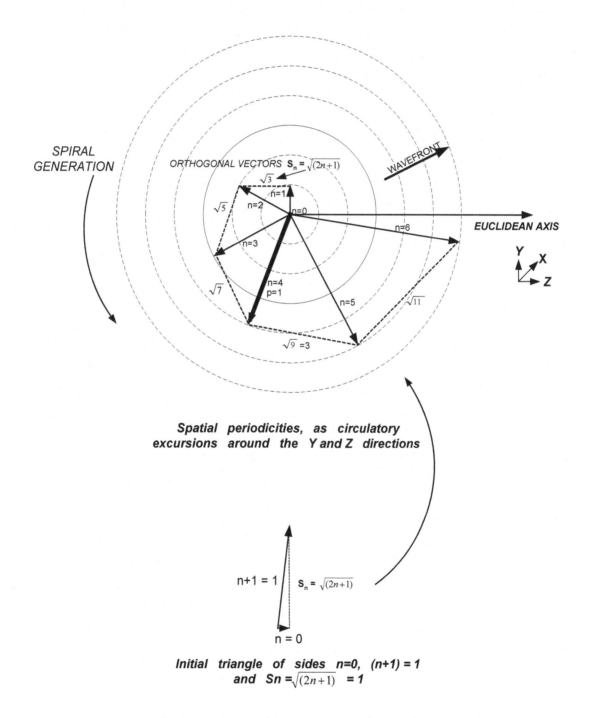

Figure 2 Spatial-periodicities in the sequence that the wave-front area-increments accrued.

A possible bundle of spatial-position periodic-modes can thus exist within the wave-front's spherically expanding surface. One spatial-harmonic mode of this bundle may then pass through apertures in, and recombine beyond, a surface otherwise blocking propagation. The process can explain the enigma of photons or particles passing through apertures, as well as various other paradoxes of relative motion.

Angular dispersion of the wave-front for a particle moving at light-speed C limits to **1-absolute radian** per quadrant, exclusively derived from the sequence of natural numbers n. One of the more general conclusions is the empirically-testable predicted relationship $X'^2 + Y'Z' = 1$ between the observed-extent along-X that gets modified by the relative motion (called X'), and the altered extents orthogonal thereto (called Y' and Z'), where $Y' = Z' = (V/C)$, with V being traditional relative velocity.

When the object moves at light-speed, it characterizes by F^2 absolute steradians of wave-front solid angle. Then, each transition from n to (n+1) occurs with $F^2 = 1$ granting zero extent (or interval) along the N-axis between the two integers. That occurs since, for the observer, no time transpires along the course of the object's motion. Its time of arrival at every next-location will equal the time at each prior-location plus the time-difference between the two locations. For the observer, everything happens to it effectively "at once." Therefore the entire wave-front formed by all consecutive integers "originate together," so that the wave-front (and spatial waves therein) comprise a zero-thickness spherical-surface without radial component.

For slightly slower motions, steradians of the wave-front diminish as $F^2 < 1$ and each transition along the N-axis would take place somewhat later (by extent or interval $(1-F^2)$. That increases the N-axis extent (or interval) for the transition between n and (n+1) and decreases the N-axis interval F^2 being bypassed for the observer. The change stems from an observer-perceived finite-timescale emerging for objects moving at less then light-speed. The object then occupies some axial-direction-thickness, at the expense of diminished solid angle steradians of excursion within Y and Z, in proportion to F^2. Parameter F^2 also gives the probability of finding the object in Y and Z within those steradians of wave-front. The probability is unity for $F^2 = 1$. For $F^2 < 1$, the probability of finding the object in the radian divergence angle within Y is F, and the probability of finding it in the radian divergence angle of Z is F. Therefore, the probability of finding it in the solid angle steradians formed by Y and Z is F^2, or $YZ = Y^2 = Z^2$, where $Y = F = Z = (V/C)$. Since the summed probability of finding the object somewhere must be unity, the "steradians" or probability affiliated with X for finding it there would be $(1-F^2)$. From figure 3, it can be seen that is always the interval beyond n at which a transition occurs.

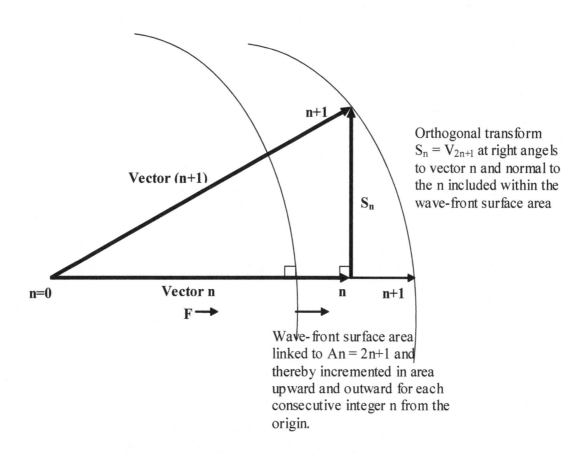

Figure 3 The interval beyond n at which a transition occurs.

Irwin Wunderman, PhD

The probability of finding the object within the origin radians specified by Y equals the length of arm F and F also equals the probability of finding it within the origin angle identifying excursion into Z. By symmetry, radians associated with direction-X should equal the length of arm $\sqrt{(1-F^2)}$ and the square of that affiliates with steradians. Partition of the unit-interval between any pair of integers along N as $\sqrt{(1-F^2)}$ and F^2 elaborate steradians within Y and Z in addition to the probability of finding the object within Y and Z. Respectively, steradians affiliated with the X-direction in addition to the probability of finding the object associated with X. As geometric parameters, F^2 and F in figure 4 graphically model physical variables of motion.

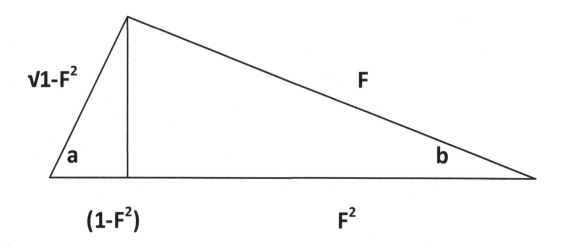

**Figure 4 Wavefront Parameters, F^2 and F graphically
model physical-variables-of-motion.**

They illustrate how shifting the location (extent or interval) between added wave-front-area-increments [with altered (V/C)] is commensurate with how time and distance would coalesce to the observer to cause such alterations. Graphically depicted F can and thus portray (V/C) making F^2 signify $(V/C)^2$. Moreover, graphical extent F = (V/C) defines either as a dimensionless numeric fraction, or as origin radians from a presumed origin point $\sqrt{(3/4)}$ above the center of each unit-diameter circle. It will be demonstrated later how, on a unit-sphere, the extent of arm F in figure 5 would designate origin-traversed-radians. The point $\sqrt{(3/4)}$ above the center of each such circle would be a distance of unity from the circle located within the paper plane and thus articulates the center of a unit sphere.

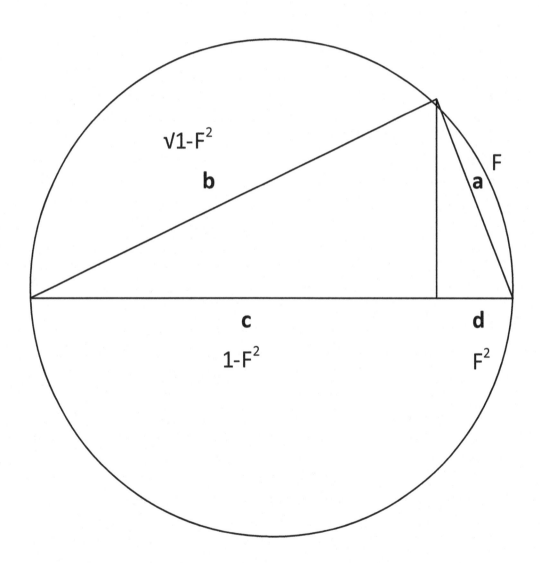

Figure 5 Arm F Designates Origin-Traversed-Radians

Since two or more observers will always be at different locations with distance between them, each observer should perceive separate time scales applicable for the other shifted by the numeric value of distance between them. For any observer, time at the other observers will be earlier than their own time for objects approaching from the other observers. Time at the other observers should be later than their own time for objects moving away from them toward the other observers. These are effects and consequences of relative motion. That difference in delayed or advanced time perceived by an observer for different directions of relative motion is one of the factors that make relative motion a distinct variable from (static distance) per unit time.

Considerations

A photon moving at light-speed moves about spatial periodicities within Y and Z as fast as its wave-front propagates. The photon and its wave-front are seemingly one and the same thing. The wave-front from a spontaneous emission at the origin is a 1-radian by 1-radian emanating spherical surface. The wave-front occupies one absolute steradian of solid angle in the form of a photon. The entire photon therefore exists within those steradians of wave-front and the possibility of finding it within that 1-steradian must be numerically the same as the 1-steradian itself, namely unity. It will be shown that an object moving slower than light-speed entails a wave-front angle less then 1-radian by 1-radian, or less then one steradian. In that case, the probability of finding the object contained within the Y and Z directions will be less than unity, and numerically equals the steradians occupied by Y and Z. Unity minus the amount of steradians within Y and Z must then equal the probability of finding the object elsewhere besides in the wave-front. A zero sum loss to exactly unity must prevail in the probability of finding the object at some location. It is known that at very small $(V/C) = F$, the probability of finding the object must be somewhere along X. Therefore, by continuity between small and large motional rates, close to light-speed, the remaining probability of not finding the object within the steradians of Y and Z must end up as the probability of finding the object along X. Conservation of total probability summing to unity must then be equivalent (or analogous) to the conservation of 1-steradian shared between Y and Z, and X.

Since for a square wave-front, steradians are radians squared, equivalent (or analogous) "radians-associated-with-X" should exhibit a squared sum-to-unity that complements the wave-front—origin—radians in Y and Z. "Radians" squared in X plus the radians squared in Y (or Z) should equal unity. Or, the "radians" squared in X plus the radians in Y (times the radians in Z) should equal unity. [Describing steradians and radians in X is metaphoric, inferring a three dimensions viewpoint versus and two dimensions, respectively]. This situation can be depicted graphically by a simple model. Since s_n represents the number of half-cycles traversed within Y and Z, (and each half-cycle comprises a 2-origin-radian perimeter around Y and Z, for $(V/C) = 1 = F$, a unit-diameter circle may be drawn between each pair of integers along the scale of s_n. Every two integers along that scale would then constitute a cycle around Y and Z (or an integer of $P = (s+1)/2$ cycles. Any two consecutive integers of S_n would entail 4-radians around Y and Z.

Figure 6 illustrates such a modeling construction. Just as extent $F^2 = (V/C)^2$ partitioned the unit-diameter circle drawn between integers n and (n+1) in figure 7, extent F^2 will similarly partition the unit-diameter circle of integers along s_n and inscribed right triangle in the upper hemisphere is then drawn. It is seen that if axial partition segment F^2 depicts steradians within Y and Z, then the inscribed arm above it is of extent $\sqrt{F^2}$ = F origin-radians that would occupy Y and Z. Analogously, the axial segment $(1-F^2)$ of the circle must portray steradians or probability associated with X because, as graphically rendered, a zero-loss-sum-to-unity of both "steradians" and probability must exist. The inscribed triangle arm above the $(1-F^2)$ need then portray the square root of steradians, or "radians-associated-with-X". The sum of [(the radians in X)² + (the radians in Y)²] must graphically and mathematically equal unity = [(the radians in X)² + the radians in Z)²] = [(radians in X)² + (radians in Y) (radians in Z)]. This graphical construction models the partitioning of probability, steradians, and radians, shared between Y and Z, and X.

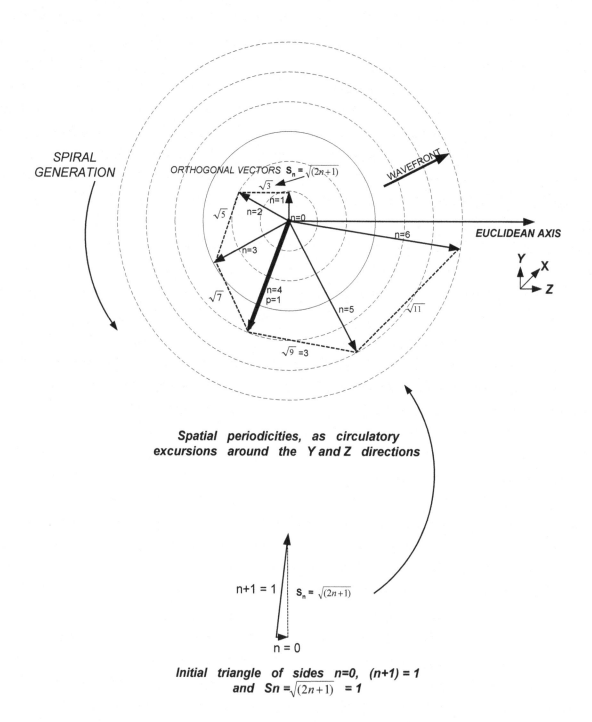

Figure 6 Any two consecutive integers of Sn would entail
4-radians around Y and Z

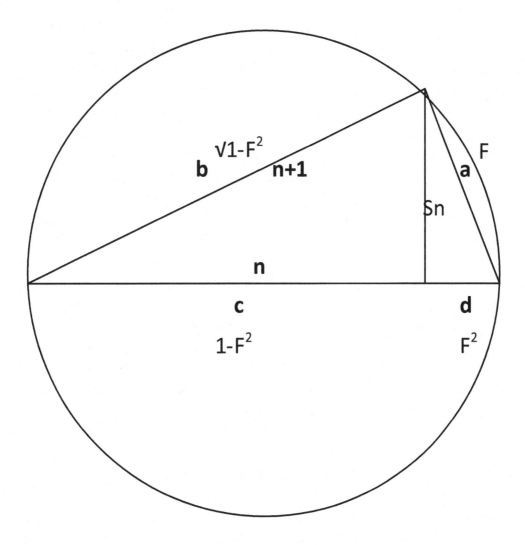

**Figure 7 Extent F² partitions the unit-diameter circle
of integers along sₙ**

Since inscribed triangle arm F is actually (V/C), how everything functionally varies with (V/C) = F can now be elaborated. For negligible relative motion (V/C) $\approx$ 0 = F. Then all of the probability for finding the object, the "steradians" and the "radians" would affiliate with X with negligible dispersive probability-wave-front occurring in Y and Z. As (V/C) = F increases, probabilities, and steradians share between $(1-F^2)$ for X and F^2 for Y and Z and while the radians respectively share between $\sqrt{(1-F^2)}$ and $\sqrt{F^2}$ = F. The picture illustrates how the wave-front grows in Y and Z at the expense of X do to its surface existing "closer-and-closer" to the object along X as (V/C) increases. For a photon at (V/C) = 1, the wave-front is exclusively within Y and Z with zero probability of finding the photon along-X. It cannot be along-X because for the observer, it consumes no time along-X due to its motion. When (V/C) $\rightarrow$ 0, the object is almost completely along-X with a minuscule wave-front in Y and Z approaching zero steradians and radians.

This can be viewed as observer-perceived conservation of radians, steradians, and probability. It can also be thought of as observer-perceived conserved localization of moving objects. Dimensionality of that portion of object which does not remain along the axial direction of approach becomes disbursed into a "comparable amount of indeterminism" in directions—orthogonal-thereto. Because only one harmonic mode within the bundle of all-those-in-the-direction-of-disbursed-indeterminism survives at termination or confirmation of the trajectory, the indeterminism remains "camouflaged" during transit. The object appears to have taken that direct path between its origin and point of termination or confirmation. The enigma of the object progressing through apertures within a blocking surface between origin and termination is explained by it being in the form of a harmonic mode during transit. None of the other possible non-surviving harmonic modes represented by indeterminism can ever be observed because they do not take place, they were potential occurrences that never materialized. The first mode to be observed or confirmed by the observer annihilates the existence of all the potential others.

The wave-front of a ballistic moving object in part characterizes where it might be. Were the real world deterministic, such that an object's trajectory could follow a Euclidean-line along X indefinitely, no wave-front need exist. The wave-front expresses an indeterminism in location. For a deterministic world, no dispersion would occur in Y and Z directions. However, when dispersion of at least the radians of Planck's constant exists, some digression into Y and Z is inevitable, even for objects perceived to be "stationary" on average. When the object acquires some minute average motion relative to an observer, it entails greater movement then when stationary on average, and the degree of non-deterministic-dispersion must increase somewhat. It should be plausible that the greater the motion, the greater the angular-digression magnifies in proportion. For example, if the effective (V/C) were 2h, one would expect the motion to be dispersive to the extent (h+h) = 2h-radians. If (V/C) were 10h, then the indeterminate-radian-angle should increase to 10h-radians. This process would continue until the light-speed, where the dispersion-angle-radians should grow to (1/h)h radians =1-radian. This describes 1/h expressible increments of (V/C) and 1/h increments of possible dispersion. That number increases with (V/C) as well as the size of each area increment added to the wave-front. Such additive area increments are representative of the mathematical "uncertainty effect" of multiple bearing directions that might occur for possible right angles taken from the direction of n-vector.

When (V/C) = F is very close to zero each ensemble of possible bearing directions only increases the angular-indeterminism-in-location of each next n-vector a minute amount. Added area-increments and resultant angle-of-dispersion are then both very small, respectively equaling 2F in area and F = (V/C) radians. The corresponding uncertainty-angle encompassed by the wave-front will additionally commensurate with F = (V/C). When F gets larger, all these entities: transition extent of the bearing-directions, added area-increment size, resultant angle-of-dispersion, corresponding angular uncertainty, and the wave-front, increase proportionally.

That porthole of uncertainty produced by the multiple bearing directions can have within its gap a potential bundle of periodic modes in addition to all the "totally random-walk sequences" that might occur. Those periodic modes "remain stable" or "sustain" over the entire course of wave-front propagation. They constitute a "path-of-continuity" to some terminal state. In a way, they represent possible "stable states" while the feasible random-modes do not repeat as a continuous uninterrupted process. The harmonic modes engender the "seeds of potential information" that may "transfer" possible locations of the moving object under the circumstances. All locations where harmonic modes exist depict possible courses of the object en route. The mathematics carries along as possible, the totality of all those waves in parallel, but only one such path will survive, or might feasibly be retrospectively identifiable when the object's trajectory terminates. In quantum mechanics that process is called "collapse of the wave function" and all of the possibilities that were mathematically carried along "disappear" except the statistical one observed empirically at whatever termination condition. The additional paths never existed as a reality, only as possibilities expressed in terms of harmonic modes. These add details to the picture that the mathematics and graphical illustrations describe.

SECTION I

THE RELEVANT ISSUES

3) Introduction

Where to begin? In basic physics, only scientific anarchists challenge conventional perceptions. Successful numerical predictions of quantum mechanics and the role of Planck's constant h are thought to be well understood. Sinusoidal representation for electromagnetic waves has been abundantly explored. Yet, the far-from-certain ideas herein have consistency, logic and elegance that warrant further discourse. This thesis purports that our interpretation of relative motion, what we call inertial velocity, is best expressed quite differently than has traditionally been done. You, dear reader, are asked to withhold judgment until surveying the full gestalt of the theory to follow.

2. This work advances viewpoints that differ from conventional wisdom. It hopes to show that:

 i. Rather than time and distance being linear, independent variables to describe physical reality, growth of **wave-front area** for a propagating wave can fill that role. Increments of spherical-surface wave-front area simulate least action paths for all possibilities as usually interpreted in the quantum-mechanical sense. That generally provides explanations for quantum physical processes. Though results are allegedly similar, by contrast, this method focuses on employing Universal Constants of Nature that are dimensionless radians, a numeric, to elucidate an equivalent picture. Here, information related to motion can take a multiplicity of possible paths between start and end points. These paths and the wave-front they comprise describe through "possibility or probability waves" or those harmonic mode solutions to the presented circumstance. This allows examining one fundamental law of Nature using a principle based on logical rationality, albeit being entirely unfamiliar.

 ii. This work contends that Universal Constants of Nature should always be dimensionless (unitless) numerics. Such constants provide the foundation bedrock for objective reality and the dimensional units that describe reality. We have historically employed arbitrary and *ad hoc* dimensional units to describe physical things but Universal Constants of Nature establish the true dimensionless standards.

Irwin Wunderman, PhD

iii. "Velocity" V of an object moving relative to an observer is traditionally treated as distance traversed per unit of time. However, distance and time apply as dimensional parameters for "almost-stationary-type-objects". They do not sustain quantitative and dimensional validity up to the light-speed. That offers one reason they are inappropriate to characterize relative motion over its entire range. This thesis exclusively discusses cases of non-accelerated or non-stimulated-emission objects relative to an observer. Analysis initially covers entities like spontaneously-emitted photons but will later extend to rest mass objects. **Work herein hopes to show that with the light-speed being C = 1, relative motion needs to be preferably described as the dimensionless ratio (V/C), rather then V = (distance)/(time)**. Relative motion is its own variable that exists in addition to the variables for "almost stationary objects" employed to delineate distance and time. **Moreover, the necessary dimensional units utilized must be those where C = unity**. The maximum rate of relative motion C designates a Universal Constant of Nature having the standard value of unity to which all other motional rates compare. The standard dimensional-unit normalizing relative motion over the entire range-of-motion is one "light-speed".

If you are one foot away from me for example, you are one nanosecond away from me; [assuming light travels at exactly one nanosecond per foot or one foot per nanosecond.] They are identical descriptions and in those units C = 1-foot/ nanosecond = 1. Here, the radian dispersion (spread) in a side length/width of the bundle of "probability waves" that characterizes wave-front location of events from a moving object proportions to (V/C). That spread is **exactly one absolute radian** at the speed of light C. **This result derives solely from first principles of whole numbers and is not dependent upon any system of dimensional units**. For smaller relative motions, the radian dispersion angle will be proportionally less.

iv. Parameter (V/C) therefore becomes synonymous with radians-of-dispersion for a side length of the wave-front that can articulate object conditions. As a measure of motion, (V/C) is dimensionless and that ratio expresses as radians, an alternative to having dimensions of distance per-unit time. Dimensionless radians apply because wave-front of the probability waves describing motion comprises a spherical surface whose two-dimensional rate of dispersion can portray via tangential over radial extents. Over the range from seemingly stationary objects to where (V/C) = 1-radian, an object's motion delineates as (V/C) radians. This radian-ratio effectively quantifies angular dispersion of the moving object's

22

wave-front. The ratio normalizes by the fastest rate of information transfer C and resulting dispersion angle everywhere tracks with (V/C). The square of that radian dispersion as $(V/C)^2$ elaborates solid angle steradians comprising the wave-front area. Wave-front surface area itself depicts all "simultaneously" possible paths and locations of the object *en route* in terms of probability waves.

v. Wave-fronts always occur in the transverse space of the axial propagation direction. A periodicity in the axial direction constitutes a uniformly-spaced repeat-occurrence of some quantifying increment in time or distance along that direction. Consecutive period and wavelength intervals will all equal each other for axial periodic cycles.

By contrast, each repeated periodicity in the transverse direction inevitably **occurs as a perfect-square function of some quantifying increment**, rather then derived from linear-increment spacing. That is because area and expanding space are a square function rather than a linear function. As portrayed by this theory and shown in figure 8, transverse direction periodicities (in wave-front areas) will always be of a perfect square type sequence. Relative motion entails the process of transferring axial information into transverse information within a wave-front and therefore involves a "mapping" from the axial direction to the transverse direction. The graphical figures of this work portrayed as spirals, cones, tetrahedrons, (V/C), and $(V/C)^2$ are manifestations of how that mapping occurs. They represent fundamental procedures to get from axial periodicity to transverse periodicity and, are thus, quite general to many physical phenomena.

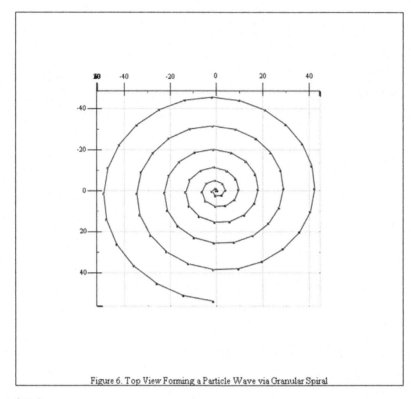

Figure 6. Top View Forming a Particle Wave via Granular Spiral

(x,y,z)

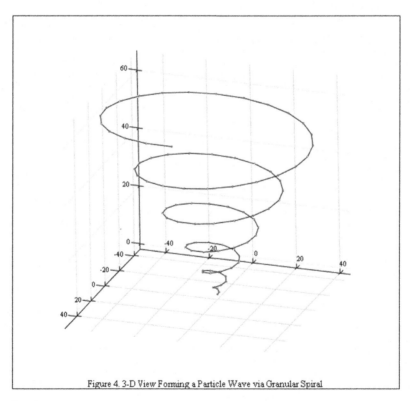

Figure 4. 3-D View Forming a Particle Wave via Granular Spiral

(x,y,z)

Figure 8 Expanding space are a square function. Transverse direction periodicities (in wave-front areas) will always be of a perfect square type sequence.

vi. This thesis hopes to show that the speed of light should numerically be absolute unity, based exclusively on the mechanism by which area accrues on the information-transferring-wave-front generated by events on a moving object. Light-speed sets its own dimensional units for all relative motion, distinct from conventional velocity defined as the ratio of distance per unit time. That precept will be repeated again and again in redundant ways in the hope of clarifying the concept. Derivation here is based on wave-fronts of possibility waves growing in area increments set by the natural number sequence of integers without involvement of any arbitrary or mathematical constants. The mathematics of this analysis is extremely simple utilizing only multiplication, addition, and subtraction of integers, plus orthogonality, squares and square roots. However, comprehension may be difficult because the paradigm is unfamiliar and abstract.

vii. Spatial patterns of consecutively accrued area increments on the information wave-fronts registering states-of-a-moving-object can propagate through space with the same periodicity as axial frequency. For a spontaneously emitted photon, that frequency is traditionally symbolized as v. In proportion to relative motion, conventional type axial-periodic-waves transfer cycles-of-axial-extent to cycles of excursion in the transverse direction, (as consecutive area patterns in the wave-front). The resultant spatial wave can subsequently propagate through apertures in the transverse direction and exhibit interference beyond. The bundle of propagating probability waves diverges from the origin object in exact proportion to the degree of relative motion, being limited graphically, mathematically, and physically at one absolute radian, which unity condition governs the limiting rate of information transfer, namely light-speed. When light-speed is unity, numerical values for distance and time become identical. For example, assuming light-speed was exactly one nanosecond per foot, objects moving toward you (the observer), are precisely one-nanosecond-earlier-from-you-in-time per foot-of-distance they are from you. Objects moving away from you are exactly one-nanosecond-later-in-time per foot-removed from you. For objects moving relative to an observer, the numerical value of time at distances from the observer will differ from the observer's time by exactly the numerical value of distance they are away.

viii. Though relative motion quantifies herein by the nomenclature (V/C), it is important to realize that this symbolism is not meant to signify (object distance per unit time)/(300 kilometers per second). That understanding bases on a ratio of traditional velocities and entails the conventional use of distance/time represented in man-made relative units. Here, the value of C is unity, and it will be shown to associate with, and derive from, the angular divergence of the transferring-information-wave-front that affiliates with relative motion. At light-speed, that solid angle constitutes **one absolute radian** by **one absolute radian** for a photon. This also represents a wave-front solid angle consisting of one absolute steradian. The term (V/C) is intended to portray the moving-object's absolute fraction of light-speed, a dimensionless numeric fraction herein called F in addition to (V/C). As such, either F or its equal (V/C), everywhere depict the fraction of a radian that the wave-front of information transfer exhibits for that respective degree of relative motion. For any (V/C), the solid angle of the wave-front would be F^2 [= $(V/C)^2$]. It will turn out that F also symbolizes properties between each unit-integer in the sequence of natural numbers. Equivalent nomenclature of (V/C) and F for the same variable are deemed justified here because (V/C) [defined with C = 1] will likely be more familiar to the reader. Graphical definitions for F and F^2 will emerge later in analysis when the case of (V/C) < 1 is treated. Since (V/C) is more readily understandable, it initially enjoys greater usage herein to describe degree of motion. Later on (V/C) and F will be used interchangeably. (see sections I and II).

ix. Radians of divergence from an origin to a spherical expanding wave-front surface will associate with degree of relative motion based solely on the sequence of natural number integers. Light-speed relative to an observer can then be defined as exhibiting one absolute radian of divergence, a limit to the possible radial divergence angle of the wave-front from the origin. That defines the Universal Physical Constant C exclusively from integers, perhaps the first physical constant to be so defined. Absolute definitions for one radian [and for one steradian] will be shown to derive directly from recurrent properties within natural numbers and not from a transcendental fraction of the 360° circle [or from a sphere of 4π steradians]. The "reason" this definition is possible stems from processes governing waveform generation and propagation. Such processes create a limit in the maximum speed of information transfer. This treatise analyzes such wave-front formation processes. One absolute radian of divergence in the wave-front represents that divergence limit for which time cannot go backward thereby restricting the maximum rate information that can transfer by a spontaneously emitted photon, for example. A rest mass particle like one of radioactive decay, will always exhibit an emerging wave-front angle less than one radian by one radian [less than one steradian].

x. Planck's constant, expressed in appropriate dimensional units, will be shown to delineate the angular irresolution of space. As alternative to a unit-of-action traditionally represented using the ad hoc dimensional units of distance and time, in proper absolute units discussed herein, it can symbolize the smallest radian angle of indeterminate dispersion that prevails along any presumed

Euclidean-straight-line. As a consequence, the smallest (V/C) of a seemingly stationary object is not zero but h-radians.

xi. In the photon-energy equation $E = hv$, Planck's constant h is the (Energy) per (cycle/second) transferred from the direction of propagation-X into the two orthogonal directions Y and Z. ("It is that simple."). As such, it is the constant that defines a minimum diffusion angle that violates perfect rectilinearity, physical orthogonality, and spatial Cartesian coordinates in objective reality. It allows interpretation as the radians produced by the possible excursion per cycle transferred into Y and Z per cycle along-X. Moving at light-speed, a photon will have fully transferred all of its extent along X to a zero-thickness spherical wave-front within the Y and Z directions. Planck's constant squared h^2, is the miniscule solid-angle-steradians of indeterminate diffusion when progressing along any direction (called X) into directions Y and Z.

xii. The harmonic exponential will demonstrate as an inappropriate function to model wave-generation in physical reality. An alternate function is proposed not devised by heuristic human concepts but based exclusively on periodic properties within natural numbers. The constants e, π, i $=\sqrt{-1}$, ∞, demonstrate as mathematically unnecessary for the absolute characterization of harmonic waves.

xiii. In equations of physics and engineering, dimensional consistency need be maintained for cycles in analogy to how dimensional consistency maintains for meters. Cycles define the conditions of repetitive overlap just as consecutive meters indicate the repeat of one meter increments. Though radians are dimensionless, cycles are not. Only within a single plane does a cycle around a circle contain 2π radians. In three dimensions, a cycle can contain any number of radians. Graphical analysis on flat paper constrains the dimensions to two, but physical reality includes three.

Often without precise mathematical proof, Section I and Section II present an overview of the analysis method. (In-depth corroboration for aspects initially over-looked also appear in two prior books[2,3]. This simpler first approach with subsequent redundancy should hopefully help substantiate the principles and assertions. It attempts to avoid getting bogged down in presenting the initial seemingly abstract logic that underpins the mathematics, which though straightforward, will be unfamiliar. The analysis in Section I addresses the motion of objects like spontaneous emission photons that propagate at the highest rate, light-speed C. Section II covers the relative motion of slower rest-mass objects. This treatise does not analyze relative motion in the presence of fields like gravity that could act on the moving object.

Various treatments herein may seem unconventional. A first non-typical characteristic is that neither distance nor time will portray a system's linear independent variable. Mechanisms of wave propagation provide the essence of this thesis. **Fixed consecutive increments of increasing wave-front area for a propagating wave** will always depict the increasing independent variable. Increments of added area for the wave-front govern the underlying process of how information propagates in space. This allows both distance and time to become variables that **depend** upon relative motion, which normalizes to the maximum rate of information transfer C. The phrase "linear-independent-variable" may introduce confusion here. Since space is square law, the area of a wave-front will typically grow in proportion to the square of time or distance from the origin. We normally consider time or distance as the linear-independent-variable of the system. In that context, the **square root of wave-front area (or a one-dimensional side-length of it)**, should proportion to time or distance. In this analysis, fixed increments of area insert into the wave-front in accord with a natural-number sequence n = 0, 1, 2, 3, 4, 5,—etc., independent of other stimuli within the structure. Since natural-numbers n provide a most fundamental linear sequence and do not depend upon other variables, they can be interpreted here as a linear independent variable driving the system. Primarily semantic distinctions may really qualify what constitutes a linear independent variable versus simply an independent variable. It should be apparent that properties of wave-front propagation for electromagnetic waves must play a key role in how relative motion causes distance and time to contract and dilate. Wave propagation mechanisms influence the perception of time and distance. Light-speed is an absolute constant because of the way waves propagate. Distance/time ratios on the other hand interpret through intuitive human concepts like simultaneity and static measurement values. Following a reference event, temporal-increment-uniformity or spatial-increment-uniformity has historically applied. This thesis utilizes **uniformity in wave-front-area-increments following an event at n = 0**.

Another atypical treatment is that if denominational units for the ratio of distance/time were utilized, they envision being such that propagation velocity (C) of electromagnetic radiation would be unity. This is not new, having earlier been proposed by George Johnstone Stoney (1826—1911)[4]. Then, distance and time describing any number of wave cycles will always be **numerically** equal. Energy-time and momentum-position will also be shown here to be alternatively describable dimensionally as cycles. Moreover, C = λν = (wavelength)(frequency) = 1 = (distance/cycle)(cycles/time) = distance/time. **Time will numerically equal distance in this format**. A Planck-length and a Planck-time should be numerically equal when the greatest possible motional rate has the dimensional value of unity.

The harmonics described here constitute diverging waves indicating possible paths. They entail information transfer. The wave-front's wave-spreading in radians describes "one side length" of wave-front area. The square of such radian-spreading, being steradians of solid angle for wave-front area, indicates probable location where the moving object might have been found, though only one wave of a bundle (one harmonic mode) will likely eventually characterize the path the object took. Quantum mechanical analogy prevails between wave function Ψ and radians of harmonic wave here, with $\Psi\Psi^*$ simulating steradians of solid angle where the object might be found. The relationship between radians and its square as steradians analogues Ψ and $\Psi\Psi^*$. This graphical analysis includes no imaginary vector $i = \sqrt{-1}$ so squaring becomes equivalent to the conjugate product in quantum mechanics. The analogy between radians and steradians here and Ψ and $\Psi\Psi^*$ should help in visualizing this interpretation. This graphical picture permits a logical explanation for what is physically happening.

As an alternative to referencing equation number, separate section numbers are employed herein so concepts supporting the expressions are proximal to allied mathematical symbolism. Certain interpretations for motion entail descriptions that differ from conventional. For example, a transition "vector" between consecutive tips of increasing-integer radial-vectors can also describe as a **path length** that can "meander" arbitrarily and **whose maximum straight-line extent is the vector magnitude**. This is a consequence of two factors. Indeterminism within the relationship allowing all possible paths to occur simultaneously, and perimeter radians swept out from the origin being primary parameters of significance. **When the path-length between two radial-vectors meanders in and out of the plane joining those vectors, it does not affect the radians swept out from the origin in that meandering**. Discussion of such subtleties in proximity of the equation can help clarify related mathematical meaning.

A further reason for using section numbers in preference to equation numbers relates to how mathematical relationships of physics usually evolve. When a new phenomenon is explored, empirical plots typically describe graphically how the involved variables relate to each other. Mathematical expressions that approximate such relationships are then used to show inter-dependencies of the variables. Physical models for those expressions that can then explain why such mathematical dependencies emerge, and these provide justification for the mathematical equations subsequently utilized. Curve fitting of at least a component of an empirically derived equation therefore constitutes the most common origin-procedure for describing phenomena subsequently referenced in text. All equations of physics that utilize exponential harmonics will be seen to be equations derived from curve fitting. The resulting equations accordingly become the primary reference upon which further analysis depends and, in text, the equation numbers reference that foundation. In this thesis, foundations emerge from the natural numbers themselves. The discussion of how that result comes about is fundamental to the analysis rather then of an empirical curve-matching origin. Resulting equations are usually extremely simple; if referenced in isolation without further address and amplified meaning, it could create ambiguity. Occasionally, paragraphs (and figures) that are further along in the book are referred to in earlier text when it was felt such information might help clarification.

The approach will examine the <u>growth in surface area</u> of an expanding spherical wave-front that incrementally grows in area by the magnitudes of radial vectors equaling the consecutive integers-n. Of the multiplicity of possible area patterns (or sizes), under certain circumstances the incrementing radial vectors can feasibly encircle the propagation direction X-axis periodically. This repetition occurs whenever the total wave-front surface area reaches an odd-numerical-integer perfect-square like 1, 9, 25, 49, 81,—etc. Analogous to least-quantum-of-action paths, repeat periodicities that occur between each pair of perfect-squares delineate possible harmonic modes in wave-front area patterns and constitute possibility waves. The situation arises solely from intrinsic perfect square properties within natural numbers and not from empirical man-made artifacts. Though these are possibility waves amongst a great totality of non-harmonic patterns, in discussing such harmonic modes the adjective "possible" will often be left out to make explanations less cumbersome.

Surface area on a unit sphere readily interprets via radians and steradians. Four equal intersecting great-circle-arcs at right angles to each other can define a spherical wave-front surface of "square-shaped-perimeter" where any side-length over unity-radial-length constitutes a radian angle ≡ (tangential extent)/(radial extent) = dimensionless. Solid angle steradians will equal (side-length squared) [or (wave-front area)] divided by (radius squared), which equals (wave-front area)/(radius squared) = $(radians)^2$ = dimensionless. Radius is unity on the unit sphere so its square is also unity and **steradians** there would numerically equal **wave-front area** while **radians** would numerically equal **side-length**. Although various portrayals for wave-front shape are possible, for graphical simplicity reasons, a wave-front's radians and steradians will often be depicted herein in terms of four such equal great circle arcs taken at right angles to form the wave-front perimeter on the surface of a unit sphere. At (V/C) = 1, it will be shown that the exterior-origin-angle of the wave-front around its entire perimeter will be 4-absolute-radians, 1-radian per side. The shape of the wave-front area can be undefined so long as the origin-angle-perimeter comprising the wave-front accrues to 4-radians per complete cycle. A circular wave-front perimeter, for example, would have 4-radians around the cone that forms the apex-angle-to-the-circular-spherical-surface.

Consider a sequence of n consecutive radial vectors called n-vectors where each next vector magnitude grows by integer increments, with n = 0, 1, 2, 3, 4, 5,—etc. These magnitudes mathematically increment the spherical wave-front surface area of a wave emanating from its source origin at n = 0. N-vector directions specify in which location each consecutive area increment is placed on the wave-front. The spherical wave-front surface is always locally-normal to radial directions of the n-vectors that begin at the apex origin. Each successive n-vector with respective magnitudes equaling consecutive integers n, (visualized as a sequence of radial extents n), increments an increase in, and quantifies, wave-front area equaling $A_n = (2n+1)$ for the spherical wave-front surface. [This applies when $(V/C) = 1$ and will later be seen in Section II to alter slightly when $(V/C) < 1$]. The 1 in $(2n+1)$ represents an initial "surface area of unity" deemed to have "occurred" at $n = 0$. This causes each subsequent wave-front area A_n to increase by 2 as n becomes 1, 2, 3, 4,—etc. (figure 9). The configuration allows the natural numbers sequence n, [or area $A_n = (2n+1)$] to be considered **linear independent variable in these analyses**.

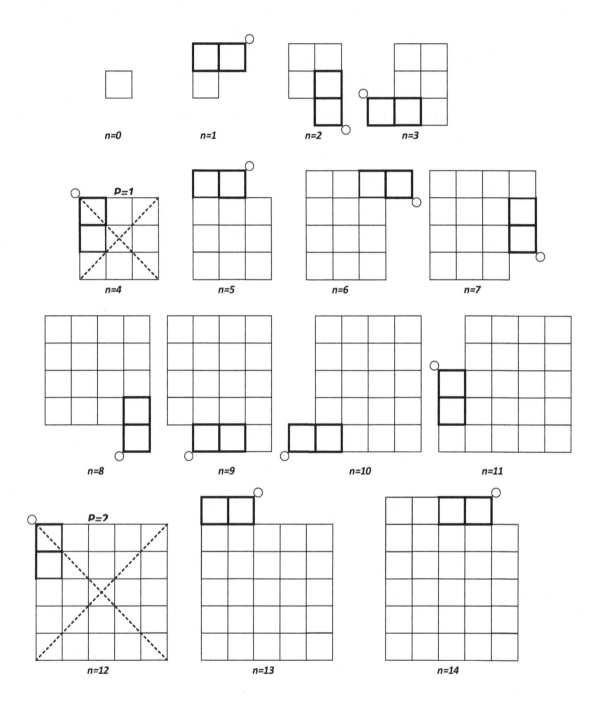

Figure 9 A portrayal of wave-front area for each concurrent nutation of n to n=14

One immediate feature of this investigation method is that propagation of information about the source origin via the wave-front will be a phenomenon that is consistent for all relative motions of source origins and for objects the wave-front might interact with. For wave-front emission from a source origin where $(V/C) = 1$, the emanation emerges whose spherical surface area grows as $A_n = (2n+1)$, with the relative motion of all other objects in the universe being irrelevant to the process. As n increases, that wave-front area continues to grow and propagate with magnitude $A_n = (2n+1)$ independent of other objects in the universe. In the case of a spontaneously emitted photon, the wave-front ultimately interacts with and is annihilated by a "detector object", deemed an observer. That could be a human eye, a film plate, an absorption molecule, or whatever. The observer perceives (in retrospect) the wave-front advancing with area increasing as $(2n+1)$ independent of the relative motion (to the wave-front) of all objects in the universe. Accordingly, a key property of photons exists whereby neither the relative motion of (or between) the source origin or detector object has any influence on the detector perceived light-speed-C between them. That independence dictates why wave-front propagating growth properties can act as linear-independent-variable in the radiative link between information-source and observer. It will be subsequently demonstrated how "periodicities" within the feasible patterns-of-growth in incremented wave-front area can transfer "possibility waves" that carry information from the source to the detector object. What we call the photon is really a propagating zero-thickness wave-front with an enormous number of potential different-sequential-area-patterns, with only a very few of them being periodic.

The circumstance can describe as the sum of the magnitudes of any two consecutive radial vectors with extents n and (n+1) always equaling the prevailing wave-front area $A_n = (2n+1)$. Each added increment of wave-front area occurs at a location locally normal to that n-vector radial direction. That sequence of possible positioning establishes the area pattern within the wave-front. Emerging from the $n = 0$ origin, wave-front surface area in direction-n everywhere equals the sum of each radial extent n plus the next incrementing extent (n+1), for the sum area $A_n = (2n+1)$. The direction of n-vector is unknown, but it must be within a fixed range of radian angles from the prior (n-1)-vector direction. It will later be demonstrated that inherent periodicity in angular location of n-vectors can occur even though offhand they may appear to all occur randomly. Such harmonic modes or multiple possible paths constitute "possibility waves" that characterize information from the moving object en route. For $(V/C) = 1$, the wave-front with harmonic-modes of area locations upon it comprise the photon itself.

Probability waves perceived under relative motion analog the cyclic "spinning" of a radar beam tracking a target as the antenna at the origin "<u>nutates</u>" about the target. The beam direction, (being directions everywhere normal to wave-front area) circulate around a central axis (call the X-axis). In characterizing wave-front harmonics, a vector simulates each radar beam direction (called an n-vector) whose magnitude from the origin here increases as the ordinal number n. Wave-front surface area will always be normal to each n-vector. **Magnitude n does not specify wave-front surface location from the origin, but as consecutive integers, n acts as the incrementing parameter to increase area in (2n+1) = A_n. In space that increases as a square law, the distance from origin to wave-front proportions to $\sqrt{(2n+1)} \approx \sqrt{A_n}$.** The square root of two-dimensional wave-front area A_n also proportions to its one-dimensional line-length, which characterizes a side of that "square-shaped area".

Utilizing fixed wave-front area increments to specify the independent variable in analyses constitutes a paradigm shift that **allows time and space to be dependent variables**. When (V/C) = 1, **wave harmonics that might result all have the specific property that the spherical surface area of the wave-front increases by fixed increments of 2 for each integer increase in n.** This stems from the area being $A_n = (2n+1)$. A unique relationship thus prevails between spherical wave-front area and the consecutive radial n-vectors that incrementally increase it. Additional factors that might further influence those fixed-increment increases might also be relevant. The direction of each n-vector emanating from origin to the wave-front will always be locally normal to that expanding wave-front surface. Each consecutive n-vector thus brings about linear independent variable information concerning **both local wave-front surface area A_n and its direction**, which area increment is everywhere normal to its respective radial n-vector.

The invariant speed of electromagnetic radiation in vacuum should make it apparent that wave propagation must influence relativistic phenomena. The property of a spontaneously emitted photon's wave-front-area increasing by fixed increments (of 2) is inferred as an overlooked mechanism. It can account for seemingly anomalous properties of light when interpreted with appropriate associated variables.

All n-vectors need not emerge co-linear along a single axial direction. They can materialize in different three-dimensional directions with some distance between their tips called s_n. Consider the transition from n to the next (n+1), to be a vector s_n, orthogonal to the 0-to-n direction as shown in figure 10.

This portrays a resultant series of concatenated right triangles as shown in figure 10a. This might seem unconventional, but it should be recognized that natural numbers n always describe "**how far each is from zero**". They do not stipulate how "far" each is from one another. The number 3 means three away from zero and the number 4 means 4 away from zero. Four does not mean one away from three!!! A more general interpretation of natural numbers does not require that they all lie along the same unique axial direction. They can depict an array of consecutive locations terminating on concentric spherical surfaces about an origin, **each surface being unity apart**

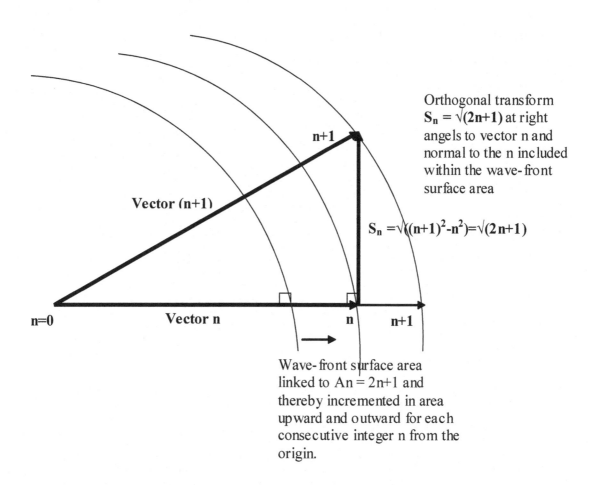

Orthogonal transform $S_n = \sqrt{(2n+1)}$ at right angles to vector n and normal to the n included within the wave-front surface area

$S_n = \sqrt{((n+1)^2 - n^2)} = \sqrt{(2n+1)}$

Vector (n+1)

Vector n

n=0

n

n+1

Wave-front surface area linked to An = 2n+1 and thereby incremented in area upward and outward for each consecutive integer n from the origin.

Figure 10 Transition from n to the next (n+1) to be a vector s_n orthogonal to the 0-to-n direction.

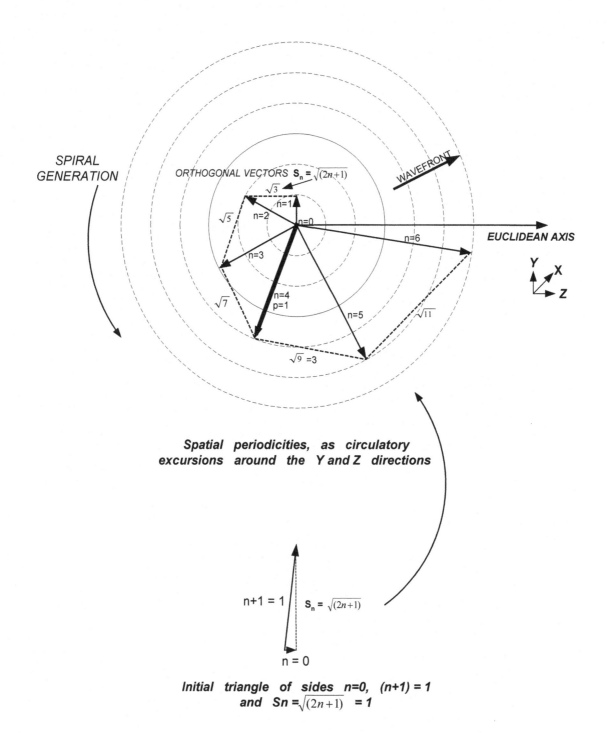

Figure 10a The resultant series of concatenated right triangles

in radius. Only for one specific condition need progression through those spherical surfaces be along a single straight-axial-line. Though that may be a common circumstance in many analyses, this thesis hopes to show it really describes only one specific limit-case of how growth in wave-front area can occur. The natural numbers can depict vector magnitudes independent of angular direction, in addition to scalar magnitudes.

Having an orthogonal non-axial component form the transition between n and (n+1) allows a broader diversity of conditions than when a priori setting that orthogonal component to zero, a condition realizable as one limit in this analysis. Resultant magnitudes and other properties of the right angle transitions will justify their use. Those magnitudes have multiple physical meanings. Orthogonal transitions existing between radial n-vector and the next higher (n+1) still requires those otherwise unconstrained radial-directions to be locally normal to the wave-front surface at respective locations receding from the origin. This is shown in figure 10a. (See previous page for figure 10a).

Each transition vector s_n normal to n (right angles to n), inter-relates that orthogonality with both the affiliated surface-area-**direction**, (i.e. normal to each n-vector), and normal-to-the area specified by n within $(2n+1) = A_n$. That allows s_n to associate with both **the transverse direction** of the spherical wave-front surface [i.e., with the wave-front's side length of the total area A_n], and with the radial **direction at that respective n**. Here, the general interpretation of a wave-front perimeter is considered formed by 4-equal-great-circle arcs at right angles. Each such side length-arc need then be $\sqrt{A_n} = \sqrt{(2n+1)}$. That happens to equal the magnitude of s_n. It will be demonstrated that one side-length having magnitude equal to s_n can be formed from a meandering path with a straight-line upper limit equaling s_n. Other variables related to s_n and to (V/C) will emerge. The _magnitude_ of each transition vector s_n further turns out to equal the square root of the sum of the two relevant consecutive n-vector's as $\sqrt{[n+(n+1)]} = \sqrt{(2n+1)}$. Wave-front surface area at n-vector is stipulated by the sum of that n and (n+1), as $A_n = [n+(n+1)] = (2n+1)$. Since s_n is normal to n while presenting a possible "vector path-length" between n and (n+1), by the Pythagorean theorem, its maximum extent will be $\sqrt{[(n+1)^2 - n^2]} = \sqrt{(2n+1)} = s_n$. It will be seen that one of the equivalent physical variables can be a meandering of that path-length of that value with straight line s_n as un upper limit. Section II will show how other variables related to s_n decrease in relation to (V/C). Because spherical surface area A_n increases as a square law of distance from the origin, s_n also happens to proportion to distance from the origin as the square root of $A_n = \sqrt{A_n} = \sqrt{(2n+1)} = s_n$. For the currently treated case of (V/C) = 1, that proportion becomes an equality and for the case considered now, $s_n = \sqrt{A_n} = \sqrt{(2n+1)}$. This immediately indicates that for this case "divergence of the wave-front" from the origin to each wave-front side-length must be = s_n/s_n = $\sqrt{(2n+1)}/\sqrt{(2n+1)}$ = 1-radian [when (V/C) = 1]. [In general, it will equal (V/C) radians.]. A proof of this was done by Jim Farned at Jfarned@rain.org[7].

Therefore, s_n links with four parameters in **magnitude** and two in **direction**. Each "side-length" of $s_n = \sqrt{(2n+1)}$. "A square perimeter" wave-front would have great arc circles as its boundary on the spherical wave-front surface. That configuration will be the most common format herein for describing wave-front area and its boundary. Namely, $s_n^2 = A_n$, which is actually a proportionality that becomes an equality for (V/C) = 1. Its **magnitude** also equals the square root of the sum of any pair of consecutive radial-vectors = $\sqrt{(n + (n+1))}$. That is how it is calculated from the Pythagorean Theorem. For (V/C) = 1, **magnitude** s_n can also equal the maximum path-length of an orthogonal transition from n to (n+1). The magnitude of s_n then also equals the wave-front's location from the origin in square law space. The two directions that can associate with s_n are the radial-direction of each n-vector, and tangential thereto, within the wave-front surface because that constitutes the direction of area A_n = (2n+1). The unique equalities of two **directions** and four **magnitudes** for s_n indicates its relevance in analysis to follow. Additionally, the variation in wave-front side-length to be later established as (V/C) leads to generic dispersion of the wave-front as (V/C)-radians. Radians of wave-front dispersion and the **magnitude** description of relative motion (V/C) will be shown to be everywhere numerically identical.

4) Insights on Causality and Uncertainty

This thesis makes a distinction between indeterminism and lack of causality in de facto physical processes. Causality connotes that some cause "must precede" (in time at the same effective place), all the eventualities from that cause. **No event can attribute to having a cause that occurred after the event**. Causality has to do with the sequence of events (taking into account delay times feasibly due to the finite velocity of light). Indeterminism means a range of possible occurrences exists that **can potentially** happen, in distinction to one specific occurrence destined to happen. The range of prevailing indeterminism permits all parallel paths to an end result to potentially occur "simultaneously" or in "parallel", although only one outcome typically results that is not a priori identifiable.

All indeterminism should be considered to have a cause preceding it precipitating that indeterminism. Moreover, it is a contention of this theory that eventualities from any cause must contain some indeterminism, however minute. That is, indeterminism can be deemed to have a "causal origin" just as all other phenomena of physics have causal origins. Such statements may involve semantics because one might argue what constitutes a cause versus natural phenomena. The issue is somewhat like the question of whether gravity has a cause. The point is raised, however, to clarify associations between causality and indeterminism. Randomness that occurs in a sequence of different eventualities can be a form of indeterminism. Empirically experienced eventualities can entail different observed outcomes containing some random attributes. However, establishing what constitutes true randomness requires a quasi-infinite number of empirical tests.

Above and beyond **real occurrences that may actually happen in pragmatic physical processes, causality and indeterminism can or cannot be present within models for physical processes**, both mathematical and otherwise. **A model for a process is hypothetical and in sharp distinction to occurrences that actually do or will transpire in real situations**. A model only has to fulfill certain elements of logical self consistency, to which reality seemingly need not comply. Models often do not exactly fit the facts. However, many mathematical models are so accurate they are erroneously considered as equivalent to the physical process they allegedly represent. A mathematical, graphical, or logical model for a physical process can exhibit either causality or non-causality. It can also contain indeterminism or be devoid of indeterminism. **Appropriate models** will however all obey (match) the rules and conditions applicable to physical circumstances by having cause precede effect and by containing some indeterminism (however minute) in representation of a physical process. They should precisely predict on paper the results that can or may occur in an actual experiment.

5) Flaws in The Harmonic Exponential Function

Use of the harmonic exponential function to depict waves and sinusoids constitutes a prime example of a currently-employed model for many physical processes that violates both causality and indeterminism. It derives from man-made synthesis for generating cyclic phenomena. The exponential mathematically generates a cyclic "frequency" that begins at $-\infty$ in time and ends at $+\infty$. This response obviously precedes whatever could have caused the generation of that frequency and thus violates causality. Even when, for example, in representation, all of the response prior to some time t_0 is deleted from use in the model, it does not alter physical-reality-violation-properties of the exponential function itself. In fact, that injects the additional mathematical violation of analytic continuity. No mathematical function synthesized to describe a physical process can change (or have any of its derivatives change) abruptly in zero time. Discarding all of the exponential function's response prior to a point t_0 abruptly alters its derivatives and as such is an invalid analytic process, both mathematically and physically. A second shortcoming of the exponential harmonic function is that it is devoid of indeterminism in its representation. It decrees that the state and course of the system can be predicted with infinite precision for an infinite time, that is, to $+\infty$ in time. No physical process can be the deterministically defined "to the end of time", however common Newtonian-type mathematical models that do so, may be.

The modeling equation for a photon's energy, $E = h\nu$, for example, includes uncertainty in utilizing Planck's constant h (a least quantum of action) in its description. Though frequency ν as cycles per second is a characterizing parameter in the relationship, **the form of those cycles per unit time is not stipulated in the expression**. The repetitive periodicity characterizing a cyclic rate need not be a conventional sinusoidal-type frequency as depicted by harmonic exponentials. This thesis hopes to demonstrate that a more general type wave description better satisfies portrayal of a photon's "frequency".

Employing an orthogonal transition between consecutive-integer-vectors has historical justification since orthogonal transitions analogously occur in the definition for the harmonic exponential function. In $\exp(i\omega t) = \exp(it/\tau) \equiv \lim n \to \infty$ of $(1+it/n\tau)^n$; the imaginary $i = \sqrt{-1}$ entails an orthogonal transition of extent $t/n\tau$ from the unity term within the brackets. Similar to the concatenated-triangles of figure 10a, **this exponential expression derives from the limit of a sequence of n concatenated right**

triangles having sides [1, t/nτ, and $\sqrt{(1+(t/n\tau^2)}$ as the number of triangles (specified by exponent n) goes to infinity. It is not possible to achieve cyclic analytic functions without orthogonal transitions (i. e., imaginary vectors). Derivation of unified waves herein does not differ greatly from the exponential function's derivation. Part of the ambiguity of utilizing i = $\sqrt{-1}$ stems from the fact that the introduced right angle can generally be **in any bearing direction**, not only in the assumed plane of the page. Nothing in the traditional exponential definition stipulates in which direction that right angle might go. This inadvertently would add indeterminacy to the function that is not included within typical analysis employing exponentials.

In this analysis, **infinite compounding of the number of triangles is unnecessary and this method yields a starting origin at n = 0 for the wave, thereby not violating causality.** Multiple possible "bearing directions" of each right angle vector-s_n also introduce indeterminism missing from the traditional exponential interpretation. That is, referring back to figure 10a, shows the concatenated-triangle's within a plane, but there is nothing that restricts consecutive triangles from arbitrarily going into and out of that plane. Actually, without the specific stipulation that all the exponential function's concatenated-triangles constrain within one plane, that function would also include indeterminism. Each i = $\sqrt{-1}$ induces a right angle forming every concatenated-triangle but there is no reason individual right angles cannot emerge within ±180° into and out of the paper plane. Without such stipulation to remain within a single plane, the exponential function need not progress around a 360° circle or even be periodic.

The definition of the harmonic exponential is essentially the limit process as n → ∞ of the concatenated-triangle graphical-configuration as shown back in figure 10a. This comes about since exp(it/nτ) = lim n → ∞ of [1+(it/τn)] [1+(it/τn)] [1+(it/τn)] [1+(it/τn)]—etc. for n terms. The product of the first two exemplary terms in parentheses would have magnitude of $\sqrt{[1+(t/\tau n)^2]}$ $\sqrt{[1+(t/\tau n)^2]}$ = $\sqrt{([1+(t/\tau n)^2]}$ [1+(t/τn)²]). Neglecting the fourth order term (it/τn)⁴ in the product, the radicand from that multiplied pair of terms will always be at least as large as $\sqrt{[1+2(t/\tau n)^2]}$. The radicand for the product of n terms would then be at least as large as $\sqrt{[1+n(t/\tau n)^2]}$. For finite n, exponential harmonics would then "grow outward" comparable to the concatenated triangles of figure 6. The drawing provides an approximate graphical representation for how exponential harmonics form as n → ∞.

Several characteristics are noteworthy about the exponential. At any finite n the right angle triangles form an ever increasing spiral. Without further stipulation about remaining in a single plane, the actual limit of that spiral at the final point where n → ∞ would be ambiguous or undefined. Nothing in the exponentials mathematical expression itself demands that each of the consecutive triangles remains within the same plane as its predecessor triangle. The imaginary vector operator $\sqrt{-1}$ effectively grants a right angle triangle arm of extent (t/τn) concatenated to each successive triangle hypotenuse, but the bearing direction of each such next right angle can conceptually be toward or away from the plane of the paper, as well as within the plane of the paper as shown displayed on a single page.

Another reason why the exponential harmonic constitutes a nonphysical mathematical expression is it contains a fundamental singularity within its description. Its mathematical definition, $\exp(i\omega t) \equiv \exp(i2\pi t/\tau) \equiv \lim n \to \infty$ of $(1+it/\tau n)^n$, effectively divides by zero as the exponent $n \to \infty$. In spite of its proliferation in science and technology, perhaps a dozen additional reasons exist[4] why the exponential harmonic function is inappropriate to portray physical processes.

A further reason subsists why the exponential function cannot appropriately portray harmonic waves. Besides lacking inclusion of some minimal uncertainty with increased time or distance, all waves must disburse in space to some degree as they progress. They cannot constitute simple unidirectional sinusoids along time or space. If such a wave existed as a "plane wave" it would contain infinite energy since it presumes infinite spectral radiance. All cyclic waves must have finite watts-per-square-meter per steradian. Neither the per-square-meter, nor per-steradian can go to zero, which would make energy density infinite, a physical impossibility. A conventional sinusoid that does not diverge with time or distance depicts a harmonic being defined as having zero steradians of dispersion, and thus of infinite energy. It will later be demonstrated that the smallest-finite-amount of dispersion constitutes Planck's constant in physical reality and sinusoids do not encompass Planck's constant within their definition. Represented without some angular dispersion, physical embodiment of such a sinusoidal type propagating wave would be impossible. Sinusoidal variations with time can typify voltages and currents within circuits, wires, or waveguides for example, but not as waves that emanate into the three dimensions of free space.

The harmonic exponential function is therefore purported to be an inappropriate mathematical function for physically representing propagating waves, photon frequencies, electromagnetic-radiation, and affiliated cyclic phenomena. An appropriate function must involve a reaction that temporally follows an initiating cause and presents a response that includes effects of Planck's constant and indeterminism associated therewith. This theory presents such a function and the waves generated are called unified waves. Analogous to the nomenclature $\exp(i\omega t)$ for the exponential, one might condense the expressions for these unified waves as $\text{wav}(PF0)$ for example, where P is the number of transpired cycles, F is the dimensionless fraction (V/C), and 0 specifies the $n = 0$ origin along X. Then, $P/2 = (s_n - 1)$, and $s_n = \sqrt{2nF+1}$.

6) The Role of Absolute Constants

Universal Constants of Nature <u>are the cornerstones of physical laws.</u> In equation expressions, they **<u>should state as a dimensionless numeric</u>**. Each will define, (in both magnitude and dimensional units), the physical-process that constant stands for. Its quantitative value sets the unit-denomination yardstick for whatever variable that physical-process depicts. Any **<u>identical physical quantity</u>** to be represented should preferably express as either a multiple of, or a fraction of, that Universal Constant. The constant's dimensional units will be absolute because they delimit the benchmark for the occurrence whose magnitude is being delineated. Entities of that constant's class have no leeway to vary. In equations, some numerical multiplier times that constant will portray the extent that phenomenon is present,**<u> in dimensional units of that standard</u>**. Any arbitrary (non-absolute) dimensional units thought to be equivalent can be assigned to that constant, but such ad hoc units are man-made, synthesized, and not necessarily intrinsic to the phenomenological process the constant specifically articulates.

The numeric value of a true **Universal Constant of Nature** utilized within equation cannot change, whatever different dimensional units the depicted variables express in. For the phenomena portrayed, such a constant represents both its absolute-magnitude and absolute denominational units. One might assign seemingly equivalent sets of ad hoc dimensional units to variables of relevance, but both sides of the equation should balance using the same numerical value in the equation for the constant. Magnitude changes incurred on one side of the equation by shifting denominational units, in those units, should exactly cancel the resultant changes on the other side without altering the Universal Constant's numerical value. Certainly a mathematical constant like the ratio of perimeter to diameter of a circle in a plane (as π) does not change for any system of dimensional units utilized. A Universal Constant means a fixed numerical constant, not something that depends on utilized denominational size for the variables involved.

It is noted that in MKS units, Planck's constant $h = 6.63 \times 10^{-34}$ Joule-seconds, while in CGS units, it is $h = 6.63 \times 10^{-27}$ Erg-seconds. This change in its numeric value immediately acknowledges that **<u>such representation is not being interpreted as a Universal Constant of Nature</u>**. True constants must be pure dimensionless numbers that have no dependence upon the ad hoc dimensional units being used. As such, they can be the ratio of any two things having identical dimensional units. In direct analogy to equation E = hν for a photon, if an expression stating x = k L, where k is a Universal Constant and L is a length, **k would not change its numerical value for length L expressed in any denominational units**. For example, if length is acknowledged in meters as L = 1 meter and k ≡ 0.1, then x = 1/10 meter. If the same magnitude length expresses in microns as L = 10^6 microns, then the equation yields x = 0.1 (10^6) = 10^5 microns, which is 1/10 meter. When the **same magnitude length** expresses in inches as L = 39.4 inches, then the equation states x = 0.1 (39.4) = 3.94 inches, which is 1/10 meter. So long as k is a Universal Constant, **its numerical value will remain unaltered for all denominational-unit systems that change, whatever units x and L express in**. The same must be true for the relationship E = hν if Planck's constant is a true Universal Constant, which it is. This analogy immediately highlights the inappropriate interpretation subsequently shown to also apply.

The differing numerical values utilized for h, as expressed in Joule-seconds versus Erg-seconds, would make Planck's constant h, **a parameter**, not a Universal Constant. One explanation for this unsuitable interpretation for Planck's constant is **neglect in preserving dimensional consistency for cycles** as h = E/ν = (energy)/ (cycles per second) = (energy-time)/(cycle). **This equation shows that dimensionally, Planck's constant is not (energy-time) but (energy-time)/(cycle)!!!** Energy and frequency must be dimensionally synonymous just as x and L must be dimensionally synonymous when k is a Universal Constant. Therefore h = (energy-time)/(cycle) = (frequency-time)/(cycle) = (cycles per second)(seconds)/(cycle) = (cycles)/(cycle) = dimensionless. Subsequent analysis will show how this ratio for h is radians, namely, a minute transferred-cycle in the tangential direction per axial-cycle.

If we describe the speed of light as 300,000 kilometers/second, it does not express a Constant of Nature because changing dimensional units of length or time will numerically alter the description. Where V as distance/time represents "traditional velocity" of an inertial observer, the ratio (V/C) by contrast is totally dimensionless and has maximum value of unity. That value of unity for (V/C) will be shown to define strictly by the geometry of integers as **one absolute radian of wave-front dispersion,** solely from properties of natural numbers. Because relative motion will be shown to entail proportional "probability" waves that "encircle" the X-axis propagation direction, (V/C) can express as the origin-radians occupied by each quadrant of perimeter of that encirclement, as well as being a dimensionless numeric. This will be elaborated, and periodicities other then those encircling the X-axis manifests in the possibility wave bundle, but examining the simplest symmetrical case should prove adequate for full understanding. As such, treating the speed of light as a wave-front having unity-radians of dispersion employs a true physical constant defined through first principles of pure mathematics, not as the result of adopted dimensional units. **Light-speed of unity will be shown as the inextricable consequence of natural number properties**. One radian per quadrant portrays both the highest rate of wave-front-divergence, and the maximum rate at which information contained within can propagate if time cannot go backward. Its derivation is "hardwired", resulting from precipitous constructions based on the number 1. It will be shown to enumerate a Constant of Nature from inherent uniqueness within the sequence of numbers.

Such limiting Universal Constants are absolute and independent of any system of units being employed. They bound the range of the relative motion parameter (V/C). Elementary graphical construction that defines the limiting speed of light as one absolute radian = (V/C) can have profound significance. It suggests, for example, the diminished likelihood of parallel universes for each different set of Universal Constants that might identify every such universe. The choice for those constants, (at least for C, an important one) is not open to selection but defined by clear and logical operation on the number-1. It is plausible that other fundamental dimensionless Constants of Nature can similarly be defined from first principles. The Genesis for Universal Constants might derive similar to C from inevitable periodicities and algorithms in the sequence of numbers. The phrase *intelligent design* of the universe might then more appropriately be *natural, consequential,* or *inevitable* design.

Physical parameters characterized by a dimensionless number can assume greater interpretive "meanings" then parameters constrained by chosen physical dimensions. A dimensionless number like six, for example, can signify six of anything while six specific dimensional-units can only be six of those dimensional units. The number six on the number scale is invariant, fundamental, and can apply to many things. Dimensionless parameters can appear far more "versatile" in equations than parameters with dimensions because they can signify number as well as denote the ratio of any two same-dimensional units. Relative motion as dimensionless (V/C) can also specify as radians, or Planck's constant h, as (cycles)/cycle) = (smallest transferred cycle to Y and Z)/(full cycle along X) = (energy)(time)/(cycle) = (frequency)(time)/(cycle) = (energy) per (cycle/second), etc. For this reason, it is plausible that various **fundamental constants of physics** will ultimately prove someday to be a dimensionless numeric, rather than be described by the relative units currently employed to characterize many physical entities. Dimensionless parameters become "**absolute**" rather than relative because they cannot change their numerical value based on the system of dimensional units being utilized in analysis. Nothing can change them, geometrically, numerically, or otherwise. They provide the bedrock of reality. They tend to have a fundamental physical origin founded on natural numbers, pure geometry, or invariant phenomena, instead of being defined through man-made relationships between parameters having arbitrary dimensional units.

7) Examining Dimensionless Velocity (V/C)

In this theory, discussion centers on the axial component of motion, the component from the moving object to an observer along the line of motional direction. A simple generalization for this seeming limitation is to assume there can always be an observer somewhere along the axial direction of motion. The analysis thereby covers all possible directions of motion. Any more complex conditions will be left to more detailed future analysis.

The maximum motional rate of information transfer (usually called light-speed C), exemplifies a *Universal Constant of Nature*. It defines the denominational-units and scale-factor for all relative motion and any quantity of relative motion should delineate as **a ratio to it. <u>It has dimensional units of motion unto itself, stated herein as one light-speed</u>**. Being a maximum possible value for the physical process, all motion should express as a dimensionless fraction in comparison to that standard denominational unit of one light-speed, or to unity. In short, the speed of light sets the units and the scale for relative motion. We historically have assigned other ad hoc dimensional units like meters and seconds to characterize the motional-process. But the ratio of distance over time is not a true equivalent to relative motion and only approximates it at very small values. Distance and time change at large motional rates. Over its full range of values, motion is an exclusive process unique onto itself. It links inextricably only to its maximum, which sets the standard, [and in a sense can register in quantized units of the smallest motion, namely Planck's constant h.]. It turns out that the divergence angle of probability waves associated with motion will track, (exactly equal) the magnitude of motion as (V/C) radians over its entire range (while distance and time do not). Therefore, units describing the diverging angle of possibility waves in a wave-front, (namely radians, being the same dimensionless ratio) can portray the motional variable as (V/C) radians.

Part of the problem in comprehending (V/C) radians as a motional indicator is that we have spent all our lives thinking in terms of seconds for time and meters for distance. At high motional rates, meters and seconds become obscure for moving objects. Their ratio fails to track their own basic dimensional definitions over the entire motional range. Those variables indicate the <u>**static or close to stationary positions**</u> of non-varying things relative to each other. That is why they are so useful and familiar to us. Motion is a separate and distinct type variable, limited by its own absolute standard, light-speed. If (V/C) describes radians, that prompts the question, "How fast is the object actually moving at so many radians? How many meters would go in a second?" We are trying to put the answer into our "irrelevant" ad hoc units. How fast it moves is not based on our arbitrarily selected yardsticks of meters and seconds. It has only to do with the absolute standard of greatest information transfer rate that we happen to symbolically label *the velocity of light C*. Entities like photons and electromagnetic radiation just turn out to have the same value we symbolically label C. If we used one nanosecond per foot as C, and the object moves at 0.5 radians, you immediately know it moves at one half foot per nanosecond (or 150,000 kilometers/second in our selected meter and second units). For any consistent system of dimensional units used for both numerator and denominator where C = 1, an object moving at 0.5 radians advances at half the speed of light. The divergence of its wave-front of probability waves will also be known as 0.5 radians. The numerical value characterizing relative motion as (V/C) **remains the same dimensionless-numeric-ratio** for any respective motional rate, no matter what arbitrary units we might use to articulate time and distance. For example, if the unit of time was the interval of 0.1 seconds and the unit-of-distance were 30,000 kilometers long (instead of the nanosecond and the foot), 0.5 radians would still characterize that motion. It would be 15,000 kilometers per 0.1 seconds, or 0.5 in those dimensional units. Motion depends only upon comparison to the absolute Universal Constant we call C, not to our arbitrary units.

Thus the ratio (V/C) with C = 1 yields an absolute dimensionless parameter for motional rate. The denominator we label as C is really *the maximum rate of information transfer* or the *greatest possible rate of motion*. It is the **standard**, and certain entities like photons and electromagnetic radiation materialize to enjoy the identical **limit.** **Those entities more rigorously represent V in (V/C), but we are so used to calling C *the velocity of light or the speed of electromagnetic propagation,* as well as *the maximum rate of information transfer*,** we will continue to use that symbolism for the standard with the above understanding. With the standard in the denominator as C = 1, the motional rate of a photon for example also characterizes as unity = 1/1 = (V/C). Meters and seconds may be acceptably-accurate for small rates of motion, but not over the entire range. Contrasting comparison to the absolute standard, for various selected sets of ad hoc dimensional units, the description of motion would not be dimensionless. It would have dimensions in those units being used. Universal comparisons as (V/C) (that can express as radians) will by distinction, always be dimensionless, while redundantly corresponding numerically to the exact radian-angle of wave-front-divergence.

The wave-front area under description might interpret as location where, during its "trajectory" the object moving at (V/C) "possibly existed" in an equivalent form comprising a bundle of "probability waves". In indicates the multiple-possible parallel paths the object could take, or could have taken, to the same resultant endpoint. It will turn out that the faster the object moves relative to the observer [i. e., the greater (V/C)], the possibility waves describing it exhibit proportionally greater potential to "spread out" from the X direction into Y and Z directions. Since the motional description can "take many paths simultaneously", they describe a multiplicity of probabilities for "landing in a given place". At high (V/C), waves of the bundle accordingly have increased ability to progress through physically separated apertures within Y and Z and interfere beyond. Increased uncertainty associated with increased (V/C) grants the moving object in its wave embodiment, proportionally greater radian spreading in its course of motion. Or, one might say, relative motion "magnifies" the minute dispersion of Planck's constant in proportion to the degree of that motion.

It is noteworthy that distance and time are not part of the nomenclature for the numeric (V/C). That represents a numerical fraction [called F] with V and C only being one set of familiar symbols useful to provide some idea of what the fraction is. The arrangement exclusively references the **absolute Universal Constant distinguishing motion** (that we historically call C). We reference that as unity herein, one light-speed. It is humans who view that absolute Constant of Nature in terms of a relationship between commonly utilized man-made ad hoc variables, nominally meters and seconds. Distance and time delineate static locations in reference to one another. The process of motion should base on the **Standard of Motion**, not on arbitrary variables defined under non-changing conditions. Relative motion should compare to the supreme and invariant motional process, particularly when that process designates through the value of absolute unity. The absolute standard of relative motion is its own defining entity. As well as indicating comparative rate of change in physical position, as radians it redundantly conveys dispersion of associated probability waves. For the maximum motional rate, probability waves and electromagnetic waves of a spontaneously emitted photon essentially depict the same thing.

The limiting speed of information transfer in the universe is possibly the most important constant of Nature. That it could avoid being the reference for all motion would be very surprising. In square law space, direct association with the order of perfect squares in the sequence of integers further raises its stature. Its high limit value, incompatible with most everyday experiences, grants no reason to overlook its importance toward explaining motional phenomena. Probability waves are an inextricable byproduct of motion. They derive from the window of indeterminism produced by the motional process. A uniformly moving object diverges as probability waves from a "route" axial to the observer to a path that spreads out at a radian angle proportional to motional rate. The dimensionless ratio (V/C) will be shown to depict the numerical fraction for that maximum wave divergence [expressed as $F \equiv (V/C)$]. Portraying the ratio as two "velocities" uses nomenclature the reader may be more familiar with, but in the definition for F, the exclusive value of unity stimulating $C = 1$ in the denominator of (V/C) is implied. If C were not unity in the representation, numerical values for spatial distances would not equal the numerical value for temporal differences at that same distance. Numerical values for the two interpretations can be the same, but for the "velocity" interpretation, numerator and denominator velocities outwardly have freedom to both express in any consistent set of dimensional units for distance and time. Dimensions within the resultant ratio then disappear and the outcome becomes a dimensionless numeric. That provides justification for using the symbolism here for a dimensionless numeric. One might then infer for example that the dimension of time within both numerator and denominator cancel, with the follow-on dimensionless ratio being distance/distance, which is the same as radians. The distinction between a dimensionless ratio of two variables measurable along a straight line, and the same numerical value in angular radians, usually is a distinction whether the system is being interpreted in rectilinear coordinates versus angular or spherical coordinates. The wave-front induced by relative motion describes in spherical coordinates, while separate V and C as velocities historically interpret in rectilinear space.

Acceleration can plausibly be treated as a rate of change in the divergence angle of the wave-front but acceleration effects are excluded from this work. Acceleration, as the time rate of change of relative motion between object and observer is not influenced by the location of, or relative motion between all other objects within the universe (exclusive of gravitational effects). Therefore, static or dynamic locations of those extraneous objects, (or whatever frame of reference they define) is irrelevant to relative motion between object and observer (neglecting gravity). Neglecting gravitational effects, spatial and time dependencies of distances between objects of the universe have no influence on the relationship concerning relative motion between one moving object and observer. But the very concept of distance is based on the static spacing between and amongst objects in the universe. Therefore, relative motion must be independent of all other spatial and temporal locations and the static or dynamic conditions amongst them. Relative motion constitutes comparison only to the absolute-maximum standard C, rather than the rate of change of distance with time. Relative motion is its own variable extraneous to distance traversed per-unit time and quantifies by the radians of dispersion of the possibility wave-front commensurate with that motion, which numerically equals the ratio (V/C). For very small values of (V/C) distance traversed per unit time becomes very close to the V in (V/C), and so that V has erroneously been assumed to everywhere characterize relative motion. Since an exact equality exists between the normalized fraction depicting relative motion (V/C) and radians of dispersion of the wave-front related to that motion, parameter (V/C) can express as radians. Being everywhere equal means they essentially are the same thing, expressible as a dimensionless value shown to be somewhere between limits of h-radians and 1-radian.

8) The Range of Possible (V/C) Values

In Section II, the geometrically-portrayed fraction-of-light-speed F will be introduced. That is the preferable parameter to describe motion. It is numerically equivalent to (V/C) and it proportionally reduces the sequentially-incremented-increases in wave-front area, from 2-per-integer-of-n at F = 1 = (V/C), to 2F. Resultant wave-front steradians of divergence then varies linearly with F. An object's motion relative to an observer, expressed as (V/C), will be noted to be equal to F everywhere. For spontaneously emitted photons moving at light-speed, the bundle-of-possibility-waves that can comprise the wave-front will be shown to diverge by **exactly 1-absolute radian and 1-absolute steradian and F will equal unity**. Proportionally less radians of wave-front divergence result for rest mass objects in accord with the magnitude of relative motion F = (V/C). Based solely on the sequence of natural integers-n without involving transcendental values, **these derivations can also serve as absolute definition for a radian and steradian**. With increased F [= (V/C)], possibility waves forming the wave-front "transfer" more and more from axial-going-direction-X cycles to transverse harmonics comprising the wave-front in Y and Z directions. Here, X is in the line-direction between object and observer. A simple relationship describing this transfer is derived for object motions that range from "stationary" to the speed of light. It purportedly expresses the Lorentz-Fitzgerald contraction along-X while including the observer-perceived "pan caking expansion" in the transverse directions. **This relationship provides a basis for prediction, and for direct empirical testing of this theory's validity or invalidity**.

The newly defined, strictly-geometric dimensionless-parameter F^2 [$\leq$ 1], later **defines through partitioning of each unit-space between area incrementing integers-n.** It has a value whose square root [$\sqrt{F^2} = F$] numerically equals (V/C). Since the square of electromagnetic-propagation-velocity C equals the product of permittivity and permeability in free space, those parameters similarly associate with unity. Then, (V/C) = F further associates with radians and the ratio $(V/C)^2 = F^2$ interprets as solid angle steradians of the wave-front, which steradians will be shown to range numerically between h^2 and unity. Many natural physical variables and constants equal unity or less in this format allowing them to additionally be consistent with probabilistic interpretations summing to that unity limit. The value of (V/C) being 1-radian at light-speed and proportionally less elsewhere, will be seen to result directly from a basic numerical algorithm of natural number integers.

It is logical that Standard Universal Constants representing physical phenomena would bound and define the range of relative motions. Unity radians describes the upper limit for progression at light-speed C. Planck's constant will be shown to delineate the lower limit, h-radians, the smallest discernible motional increments. The separate fraction-F variable can express all motion as $F \equiv (V/C)$, applicable over the range $h \leq F \leq 1$, while associating with angular divergence of F-radians for probability waves that portray that motion. That characterization applies to these discussions and indicates simplicity of the configuration.

In a sense, motion as $(V/C) = F$ might perhaps be thought of as a "parameter" supplementary to space and time. Motion has its own minimum and maximum limits and actually dominates (can alter) perceived space and time. Motion is rather extraneous to static locations within space and time that we use for orienting fixed things relative to each other. When objects move, they no longer "fit" into that static structure. However all entities move relative to each other, with the appearance of being stationary just an illusion of averaging. As a norm then, motion is likely a condition or circumstance unto its own characterization. If I am within an enclosure where everything is stationary relative to everything else, all objects possess fixed space and track in time-sequence dimensions. That applies for me and amongst all other objects therein. When I move relative to those fixed surroundings, dimensions between objects in that enclosure change for me, and I change for them, but none of the others change in relation to themselves. Therefore, my relative motion is something separate and apart from the other fixed dimensional units that base on meters and seconds. My motion has its own separate absolute universal limit C, which is virtually irrelevant to other objects within the enclosure if they remain fixed. Accordingly, it appears reasonable to consider motion as and entity in its own right, rather than to intermix it with other arbitrary units based on distance and time.

9) Planck's Constant Interpreted as Dimensionless Radians

Cycles need to be being dimensionally accounted for when checking dimensional consistency. The designation (energy-time) per cycle is not dimensionally equivalent to (energy-time). A cycle constitutes the dimensional units of a complete advance to a fixed repeated point, one cycle later. It is analogous to a meter that dimensionally denotes linear advance to a fixed point one meter advanced. On the other hand, a radian specifies the ratio of tangential-distance-progression to radial distance. It is considered dimensionless, but has transference implications of (tangential)/(axial) or orthogonal to/axial. Whether that transference property of motion truly leaves them "dimensionless" is a somewhat semantic issue, but they will be referred to as such herein, for traditional reasons. **The two dimensional distances being ratioed are not confined to remain within the same plane**. There are 2π radians to one rotational cycle of a circle for example, only when that rotation takes place within a single plane. There can, for example, be 8-radians for a given cycle, if, for sustained unit-distance from the origin, the tangential path were an elongated rectangle or arbitrary "path-length" having a perimeter of 8-radians. Radians can be, and often signify **three-dimensional**, seemingly dimensionless constants amenable as Universal Constants of Nature.

The photon energy equation $E = h\nu$ is a convenient example of a modeling equation for a physical process where Planck's constant h dimensionally represents (energy-time) per (cycle), or (energy) per (cycle/second), or cycles per cycle, or radians of dispersion. This thesis hopes to elucidate how dimensionless denominations of cycle-per-cycle or (energy-time)/cycle, or radians-of-dispersion all invariably apply to h in this circumstance. In presentation, graphical renderings are used extensively to help visualize the new unfamiliar formats. In spite of the seemingly elaborate procedures used here to describe and then mathematically prove this preferred method of wave modeling, the resultant function can be depicted by simple symbolisms analogous to $\exp(i\omega t)$.

Portrayal here interprets Planck's constant h to be a dimensionless **Universal Constant of Nature**. It symbolizes the **minimum angular-indeterminacy** within space-time and the minimum un-resolvable divergence of a wave or probability wave. All physical variables possess a "noise level" or limit of resolution and Planck's constant represents that limit for geometric spatial delineation. In human ad hoc dimensional units, it can also **equal the minimally obscured energy-time product tangential**

to the axial propagation direction for one cycle of wave. The latter interpretation utilizes arbitrary dimensional units such as currently employed MKS or CGS. To appear as dimensionless radians under this theory necessitates absolute dimensional units as will be further elaborated.

Parameter h can graphically describe in terms of radians, (tangential cycles)/(axial cycle) or (tangential-length)/(radial-length). It can also be the smallest-possible value of (V/C), so that $h \leq (V/C) \leq 1$, which remains dimensionless throughout the entire range. This lower limit analogues the quantum mechanical interpretation where each elementary particle maintains a Planck's constant least-quantum-of-action $h = \Delta E \Delta t$ in its energy-time product. **This relationship for dimensionless (V/C) characterizes all motion between the bounds of two Universal Constants**. They are light-speed C = 1as maximum, and Planck's constant = h as minimum attainable. **Those Universal Constants of Nature had fitting values proposed by Stoney and Planck[5] more than a century ago.**

In the photon energy equation $E = h\nu$, Planck's constant h is the (energy) per (cycle/second) transferred from the direction of propagation-X into transverse directions Y and Z. As such, it defines the minimum "diffuse" dispersion that violates, spatial orthogonality, and Cartesian coordinates. Planck's constant might be thought of as perhaps due to non-localization of the smallest elements of matter. These elements all move relative to each other with intervening forces between them. Their exact locations are not determinable, as in the many-body problem of movement. When the scale of examination becomes more and more macroscopic rather than microscopic, an increased **ensemble of particles** can appear "**stationary**" relative to another **averaged ensemble**. However, a "fuzziness" associates with where any individual smallest element may be, and such diversity in position due to motion reveals a minimal radian angle of uncertainty called Planck's constant. In developing the black-body radiation-emission-relationship Planck himself attributed the constant to many separate "oscillators". The inability to articulate discrete specific positions in the realm of those oscillations conjectures to create the resolution limit $(V/C) \geq h$ on all motion.

Traditionally, Planck's constant h, represents a least-quantum-of-action, dimensionally interpreted as energy-time, momentum-position, or action. How can this understanding reconcile with h as a dimensionless fraction for smallest (V/C)? Consider the wave description for h as it appears in the photon energy equation $E = h\nu$. Here h symbolizes photon energy E divided by photon-frequency ν. If h were a dimensionless fraction, energy and frequency would be dimensionally synonymous, e.g., $E = k\nu$ where k is a dimensionless constant. Then $h = E/\nu = $ (energy)(time/cycle) = (frequency-time)/(cycle) = (cycles/time)(time)/(cycle) = (cycle)/(cycle), which is dimensionless and will be shown as equivalent to radians. It also describes the smallest discernible value (V/C) can have. Here, the numerator would be a cycle of extremely small excursion (associated with the smallest distribution of indeterminate wave incursions into Y and Z directions), compared to one full cycle along-X delineating a denominator of unity. That ratio is dimensionally (cycles)/(cycle). Stated in this format, Planck's constant becomes absolute, a dimensionless numeric Universal Constant of Nature independent of man-made dimensional unit-scales for energy, time, momentum, or position. In terms of traditional units it could be (energy-time in Y and Z)/(energy-time in X). Both times could then cancel and the numerator represents energy in Y and Z compared to the denominator-energy-term along X. The numerator term forming the radians of Planck's constant (when one denominator cycle applies) signifies the smallest amount by which energy interchanges from X into Y and Z. Namely, it would denote the quantum of energy or the least quantum of action or the "smallest amplitude" bundle of cycles that can transfer from-X into Y and Z directions.

Action can be deemed to denote a tiny **tangential-excursion-cycle**, transferred per axial cycle. When the frequency of that cycle is high, the time-period represented by it is short and vice versa for all frequencies. For any given cycle, the product of (frequency) (time associated with that cycle) **will remain constant for all frequencies**. That is why h can be constant. The same small excursion cycles as (energy-time) = (frequency-time) will be invariant, being interpreted as a unit of action. Planck's constant h identifies **the smallest discernible radians around the perimeter of a cycle, or excursion into Y and Z per full 4-radian-perimeter-axial-cycle along X.** It also represents as [(cycles disbursed in a transverse direction) per (one axial cycle)], **or as radians**. Accordingly, it indicates the inherent limiting angular-description of space as the prevailing radian angle of uncertainty in any given direction. It portrays the minimum angular spreading with distance of an otherwise presumed Euclidean straight line. Its square depicts the minimum steradians of dispersion with progression in any direction.

Such a ratio for h, as a very small dimensionless number is consistent with the equation E = hν. It seemingly presents a problem because the familiar numerical value for h historically interpreted as energy-time. That understanding depends upon the dimensional units utilized for energy and time rather then being a constant. Those conventional-interpretation units are arbitrary, (e.g., E = ergs, or joules, or what ever) and that is the problem. In that form there will be seemingly appropriate sets of dimensional units that can make h come out whatever numerical fraction is desired, **while still representing precisely that same physical magnitude of energy-time, (interpreted in whatever ad hoc units were used)**. When h has cycles in its denominator as energy-time per cycle, (as it should) only a specific absolute numerical fraction portrays the result. This thesis contends such absolute units are necessary. They represent a real **radian angle of indeterminacy for space**, so h can thereby describe a tiny transverse-excursion-cycle per axial-cycle in those absolute units. The appropriate absolute units are not assuredly known at this time because the exact radian angle of dispersion represented by Planck's constant remains unidentified. Were the numerical value for electron charge e assuredly defined for dimensional units where C = unity, we might guess from the fine structure constant that the radian angle for h = $(2\pi137e^2)$ radians $\approx 2.28 \times 10^{-35}$ radians. This numerical value in radians is about 1/30 the numerical value of Planck's constant in MKS units of Jules and seconds. Were the above supposition valid and C = 1, suitable for Jule and Second dimensional units, choosing ad hoc units of Jules and Half-minutes would (for this presumed example), result in a preferable **numerical value** for Planck's constant that more closely **matched the actual Universal Constant radian angle**. In those Jule and Half-minute dimensional units, the quantitative magnitude of an energy-time/cycle represented by h would be **unchanged** from what is currently utilized in MKS units.

Interpretation of Planck's constant h as the minimum radians of dispersion of an otherwise presumed rectilinear straight-line-ray grants a limit of visibility regarding information within small places. **An uncertainty of h-radians stipulates a Planck length of distance-uncertainty on a unit sphere**. On the unit-sphere of time, it is also numerically the same as a Planck-time. Quantitative discrimination within angles less than h-radians, as well as for distances less than a Planck length, and time less than a Planck-time become impossible. Similarly for solid angles or surface areas less than a (Planck length)^2 = h^2 and within volumes bounded by surfaces of h^3. Empirical experience seems to corroborate these limits. They imply an absolute physical angle of h-radians subsists beyond which Cartesian coordinates and rectilinear space cease to be valid models for reality. The precise angle remains somewhat elusive at this time. Such interpretation is perfectly reasonable and signifies a "noise level" in "direction precision" beyond which finer measurements cannot be made. It holds that resolution limit in the form of a radian angle, which manifests dimensionally as (energy-time)/(cycle) = (cycles)/(cycle) in the E = hv description for a photon. Relative motion between two seemingly stationary objects is traditionally considered zero. However each sub-constituent particle comprising an object is never really "at rest" with respect to any other constituent particle on any object. All elementary particles move relative to each other even when the average position of the ensemble that comprises one object is considered stationary compared to the average position of another ensemble of particles. That depicts the sub-dynamic condition we call at rest. **Since relative motion only defines between de facto entities (actual smallest particles) that articulate in time and space (not between some-fictitious-average non-particle-occupied positions conceived by humans at a hypothetical location within space), true motion as (V/C) = F can never actually "go to zero", even between seemingly stationary objects**. At least some effective relative motion (V/C), however minute, must prevail between any particle and another "observer particle".

56

It could be described by a very small dimensionless fraction, or a small number of origin radians of dispersion. Such minute-average-motion would make any other object appear "diffuse" by that small number of radians. This thesis contends that such smallest motion is characterized by Planck's constant h. Since the minimum (V/C) = h-radians, it implies that the traditionally expressed minimum velocity stated as distance/time would equal $V_{min} = hC$. That velocity V_{min} would be the radian-fraction-h of the largest "Velocity-C". Offered in the traditional format of a Velocity-V as distance/time, may make it more readily understandable how the full range of relative motion (V/C) covers $h \leq (V/C) \leq 1$ radians. It can also be stated as the origin-radians around the perimeter of a dispersion possibility-wave-front created by relative motion will range between 4h-radians as 4-radians.

It is reasonable that Planck's constant should depict the limiting angular resolution of space. It symbolizes the smallest discernible radian-angle of uncertainty. When discussing the cycles of any frequency, for example, it articulates the minute fraction of a cycle that might occur in a transverse tangential direction for one full cycle that transpires in whatever axial direction. It thus has dimensions of cycles-per-cycle, or is dimensionless. Because the angle is so small, it can also demarcate in terms of radians. To be redundant, in the photon energy equation $h = E/\nu$ for example, energy and frequency are dimensionally synonymous, making h a dimensionless constant irrespective of dimensional units employed. Here, using time units of seconds, (energy E)/(frequency ν) = (Planck's constant h) = (energy)/(cycles per second) = (energy x time)/cycle = (frequency x time)/(cycle) = (cycles/second)(time)/(cycle) = (cycle)/(cycle). For one axial-direction-cycle of denominator frequency ν, the **numerator**, as a diffuse "smallest-transverse-cycle" of frequency E in the tangential direction is dimensionally equivalent to (energy-time) = (frequency-time) = (cycles/second) x (time) = (cycles). A **numerator to denominator ratio** of any two dimensionally identical parameters, particularly where the denominator represents unity denomination, could allow Planck's constant to be interpreted as a multiplicity of dimensionless numeric ratios.

10) Wave-front Area Increments as the Independent Variable

What does it mean to describe wave-front area incremented by consecutive-integer vector-values-n, rather than the traditional scalar representation for area? Spherical wave-front area has a **magnitude and a facing direction away from a point of origin. As an area, it comprises vector information with two relevant components encompassing both magnitude-of-area and facing-direction, plus the natural number sequence for incrementing area increases.** Facing direction from the origin is invariably everywhere normal to the spherical surface area. That direction associates with, and differs at every integer-n, wherever its associated radial-n-vector-direction may be. That description encompasses the incrementing method employed here. Since space itself and wave-front area increase as a square law away from an origin, the square-root of wave-front area (often as wavelength-distance, time-periods, or s_n traversed half-cycles from the origin) delineates **location** of the progressing wave-front. Wave-front area should proportion to the square of such distance, time, or cycles from the origin. As part of a spherical surface, it would locate at positions normal to (and somewhere along) each respective n-vector direction, as well as being normal to the central X-axis; namely being locally normal to any radial vectors from the apex origin facing outward toward the spherical surface area. Those radial directions identify the direction and sequence in which each element of the wave-front surface area advances.

A distinction involves what constitutes the independent variable or linear independent variable for the function. For the exponential, it is time t. When n is small and finite each unit-increase in n would create a large incremental change in the net product for any specific value of t. Resultant increments would then be "course and granular". As n becomes ever larger, each unit increase in n implements a smaller and smaller percentage change in the resultant product for any given time t. Time t tends toward becoming a continuous variable as $n \to \infty$ and that continuous variable is presumed to advance tangentially around the unit circle.

For the unified wave of figure 11, the independent variable is **wave-front area, in sharp distinction to being time t**. At low n, the **percentage change** in area with each unit increase in n is similarly large, associated with the change in $[2/(2n) = 1/n$. Though n need not approach or equal ∞, **here the independent area variable also tends toward becoming more and more continuous at large n**. Near larger n, unit increases in n will have ever smaller influence concerning percentage increases in wave-front area. To simulate physical systems where changes occur close to continuously, investigative regions near large n constitute the relevant circumstance for both the exponential and unified wave. While the concatenated triangles are graphical analyzed at relatively small n for pragmatic visualization purposes, large n conditions (as in the exponential) portray the real-world. In a propagating wave, we interpret wave-front area to grow essentially "continuously". Thus, **<u>the primary region of interest for the waves being analyzed will be toward large values of n</u>**. There, all cycles and quadrant divider locations tend toward having **one absolute radian of separation**, each quadrant describing exactly ¼ of every full cycle.

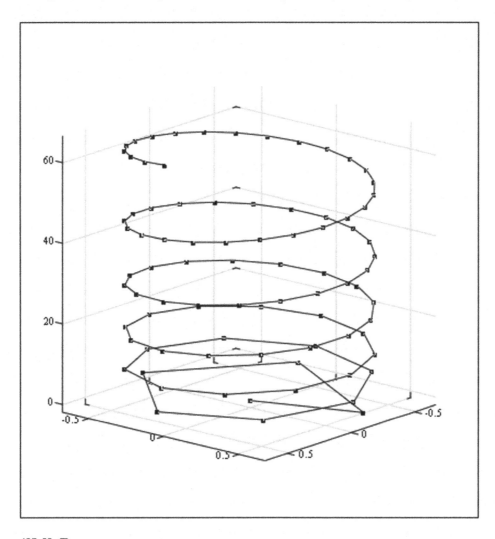

(X,Y,Z)

**Figure 11 The unified wave independent variable is the wave-front area
(each point is the end of vectors n, n+1 ... so on)**

This work utilizes an uncommon method to describe how a wave-front surface area grows. Information transferred within the universe between an event and observer occurs via the mechanism of wave-front propagation. Analysis of that mechanism is therefore fundamental in understanding rules of Nature. The method involved effectively considers each incremental increase in wave-front area as a "new" state of the system. Such states are represented by the natural number integers n = 0, 1, 2, 3, 4, 5,—etc., where total prevailing wave-front area will be seen to sum to $A_n = F(2n+1)$. Section I herein considers the case of F being unity, so in $A_n = (2n+1)$ each integer increase in n establishes a next-system-state with area incremented 2 units greater than the predecessor state. A graphical picture showing how, from an origin event, wave-front area increases by incremental insertions of area 2 is perhaps most easily described by crude analogy to the possible directions of a Foucault pendulum.

Figure 12 displays the "possible random walk" directions taken by such a pendulum. The analogy is not with respect to processes of simple harmonic motion or to gravity pulling on the pendulum. It is to reference feasible directions of an n-vector from an origin.

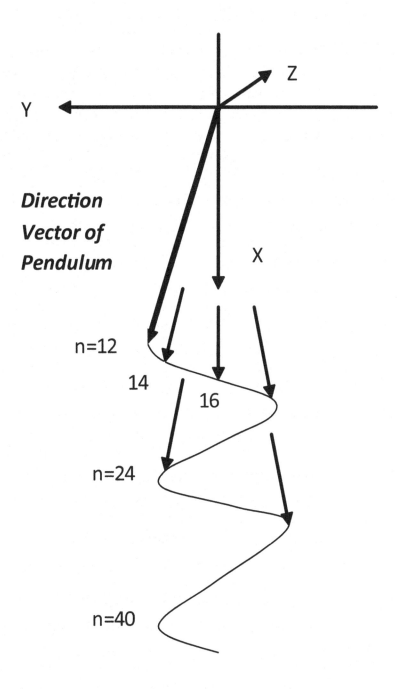

Figure 12 Possible "random walk" directions of a Foucault pendulum

The picture differs from a conventional pendulum since each consecutive n (simulating the origin to hanging-weight distance) grows by unity compared to its predecessor. As vector direction from the origin changes, the magnitude of the n-vector continually elongates in proportion to n. Area of the wave-front surface would grow as $A_n = (2n+1)$. While the X-direction points downward in this illustration (to simulate analogy to a pendulum) such direction would normally be between the wave-front's origin and the observer. It is important to recognize that **n is not the physical distance connecting wave-front and origin in the model employed by this theory!** [**In square law space the origin to wave-front distance would typically proportion to the square root of wave-front area, or to a one-dimensional side-length of that area**.] The pendulum illustration and analysis is meant to depict possible consecutive directions of inserted incremental areas when establishing the total wave-front area $A_n = (2n+1)$ at that value of n. The direction of the vector from the origin tells where the new increment of area might be inserted, and the magnitude of n, [when substituted in $A_n = (2n+1)$] tells what the total area is at that n. The expression "might be inserted" is necessary because the exact direction of insertion elaborates as indeterminate.

Under those conditions, all possible "adjacent locations" to where the pendulum currently is at are feasible for inserted area increments, and they must all be treated as "simultaneously possible" and carried along mathematically as "parallel possibilities." Insertion locations can "all occur in parallel" so to speak, though there exist constraints on how far tangentially [and axially] each new insertion increment of area 2 can be from its predecessor. This tangential restraint might be considered analogous to the length of each step in a random walk. The maximum allowed tangential extent of each step will be explicitly defined herein, but that maximum extent can comprise from any "meander-line" which has the same cumulative limit-length as the straight-line maximum. The step can be as small as close-to-zero and as great as the straight-line maximum. All of these conditions represent possible circumstances of how wave-front area can grow with each n delineating a newly specified feasible-state-of-the-system. Almost all the quasi-infinite number of potential-consecutive-states-and-conditions that can apply will be totally random. A very few of that total can exhibit inherent periodicities in sequence and location-direction, and analysis herein intends to articulate how those periodicities come about. Those "modes having directional repetitions" and periodicity in area increments can transfer a harmonic pattern within the propagating wave-front. Such bundle of cyclic patterns can allow information passage and subsequent interference of a periodic mode through apertures in the wave's pathway between origin and observer. A cyclic mode of those periodicities within the wave-front can traverse a pair of double slits in a rigid surface seemingly blocking the wave-front, and recombine beyond to constitute a single-observed detected-mode from the enormous array of possibilities that existed. This treatise derives circumstances for viably transmitted cyclic modes and the consequence of their existence.

This theory can infer a slightly altered interpretation of how space progresses as a square law when advancing away from an origin. Whenever an origin-concentric expanding spherical-wave-front-surface with an area $A_n = (2n+1)$ numerically reaches an odd perfect square (like 1, 9, 25, 49, 81, 121, etc.), **<u>another cycle from the origin will have transpired</u>. The square law of space will be seen as describable in terms of perfect squares in the spherical surface area of an expanding wave-front.** Alternatively, this occurs whenever $s_n = \sqrt{(2n+1)}$ is an odd integer.

11) Integer Radial-Vectors-n Increase Wave-front Area As $\sqrt{(2n+1)}$

A spherical wave-front's surface area has greater "dimensional interpretation" then an area depicted as (length)^2. Every point on the wave-front divulges an associated vector direction emanating from the point of wave-front origin. **That vector direction comprises descriptive information about the relevant surface area. For modeling, a vector sequence emanating from the origin, having consecutively increasing integer magnitudes n can increment the way wave-front grows, with each surface area locally-normal to the vector direction and proportioning to magnitude n.** "Correlation" will then exist between every proximal element of prevailing area and its radial direction from the origin. Such correlation can also encompass the consecutive sequence in which those prevailing areas were compiled. Sequential vectors emerging from the $n = 0$ origin must all occur locally normal to the wave-front surface, whatever the angular distribution of those vectors. They increase in magnitude integer-by-integer and are called n-vectors. Certain circumstances grant periodic directional repetition of those n-vectors around the X-axis, and those harmonic-modes are of particular interest here. The case of periodicity that surrounds the X-axis is treated for its symmetrical simplicity, but periodicities surrounding any and every n-vector are possible and constitute the total wave bundle of possible harmonics.

Under generic conditions described herein, vectors n, and (n+1) from the origin, and transition extent s_n between them form a triangle envisioned for the moment within a single plane, and s_n will have magnitude $\sqrt{[(n+1)^2-n^2]} = s_n = \sqrt{[2n+1]}$. (See figure 1 and figure 2). Each transition extent to the next higher integer thus also constitutes the square root of the sum of the relevant pair of adjacent integers n and associated (n+1), i.e. of $\sqrt{[n+(n+1)]}$. Full cycles will occur between the perfect squares of $A_n = (2n+1)$, or between the odd integers of $\sqrt{(2n+1)} = s_n$. Since s_n represents something at right angles to n-vector, [and magnitude-n also increments and expresses within wave-front area $A_n = (2n+1)$], s_n can depict parameters at right angles to wave-front area A_n. Accordingly, it can portray distance, time, or number of transpired half-cycles [odd integer square-roots of the cyclic perfect-square in (2n+1)] progressing along axial-propagation-direction-X. A spherical wave-front will have its distance from the origin somewhere along and normal to each n-vector at the same distance that wave-front exists along direction-X. Since s_n is also at right angles to n-vector [the normal from origin toward wave-front area] it could portray something at right angles to radial n-vector.

That could be "parallel" to and within the wave-front surface and hence tangential to n-vector. Namely, it could signify the extent of one "side-length" comprising that area if that spherical wave-front area were of "square shaped perimeter". The many equivalent numerical values of s_n that have different meanings will each be given an additive subscript to s_n to distinguish that meaning.

Using the topology presented above, it has been mathematically proven that periodic harmonic modes are feasible for values where area $A_n = (2n+1)$ is a perfect square, i. e., where $A_n = 1, 9, 25, 49, 81, 121$,—etc. There, $s_n = \sqrt{(2n+1)} = \sqrt{A_n}$ equals the consecutive odd numbers, 1, 3, 5, 7, 9, 11,—etc., for n = 0, 4, 12, 24, 40, 60,—etc. respectively. Values of n where $A_n = 2n+1$ is a perfect square and $s_n = \sqrt{(2n+1)}$ is an odd number, graphically render on the spiral in figure 2 as n-vectors with **partially-broadened radial lines**. Though all triangles are illustrated within the same paper-plane, nothing constrains the directions of consecutive-triangle-planes relative to the planes of prior or later triangles. These circumstances and their continuation outward delineate each consecutively-outward perfect square in $A_n = (2n+1)$, from n = 1 toward n → ∞. Namely those conditions specify where $s_n = \sqrt{(2n+1)}$, becomes each next-higher-odd-integer. Such values of n delineate every sequential perfect square circumstance describing area $A_n = (2n+1)$.

Since each consecutive odd-number-value for s_n signifies one transpired cycle, magnitude s_n numerically indicates the number of prior half-cycles from n = 0 to reach area $A_n = (2n+1)$. It will be further demonstrated that those magnitudes of n delineating possible cycles distinguish where radial n-vectors encircling the X-axis in three dimensions can periodically overlap. As concatenated triangles in different planes undergo consecutive intervening cycles about the origin, those specific perfect square n-vectors would all return to overlapping coaxial directions when a periodicity occurs. The result is that radial-n-vectors can periodically spiral around a conical surface **to cyclically reach repeated directions** at all perfect squares of (2n+1). See figure 13.

This might not depict the only harmonic case, but it is initially presented for ease of illustration. The spiral drawing serves as a "skeleton" to show how periodicities could occur.

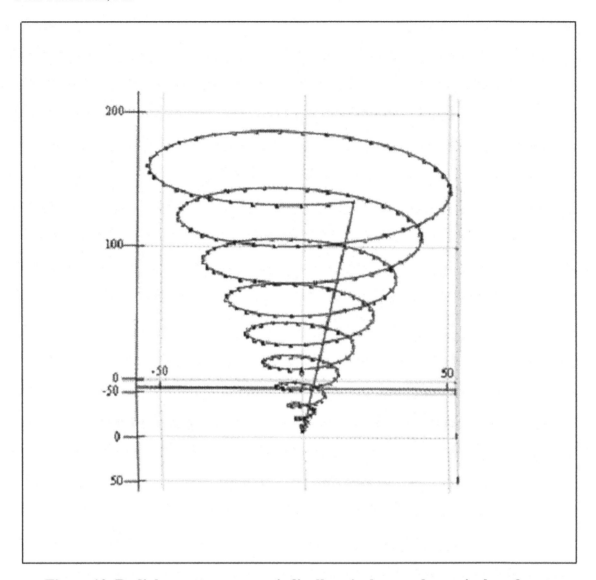

Figure 13 Radial-n-vectors can periodically spiral around a conical surface to cyclically reach repeated directions at all perfect squares of (2n+1).

Figure 2 outlines one possible description within a single plane of how n-vectors might emerge from the origin. With associated straight transition vectors s_n they appear as a sequence of concatenated right angle triangles, each having radial extent n one integer greater in length than its predecessor. The n-vectors render here within the plane of the page. In three dimensions, the triangles might form most any zigzag interconnected external shape in addition to the one shown within the paper plane. They could form to have a square-shaped external surface with four identifiable sides as in figure 14.

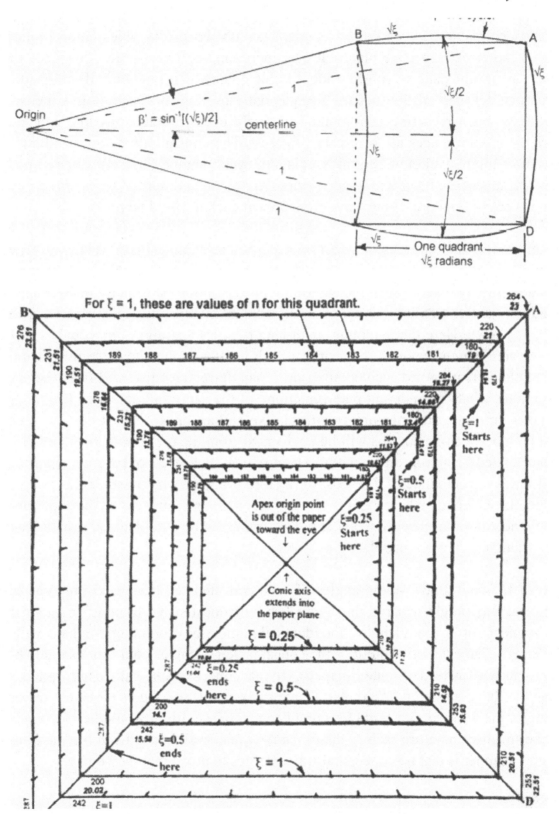

Figure 14 The n-vector sequence then forms a periodic pattern with four identifiable quadrants if (and only if) all quadrant directions (corners of the "square") sequentially overlap in direction as n increases endlessly.

Under periodic mode conditions, overlaps within those four sides could replicate within the same respective planes at ever increasing-n. The n-vector sequence then forms a periodic pattern with four identifiable quadrants if (and only if) all quadrant directions (corners of the "square") sequentially overlap in direction as n increases endlessly. Such recurring conditions will rarely occur, though **possible** and those periodic circumstances are of greatest interest. The configuration suggests how the n-vectors might encircle a central X-axis in a cyclic matter. For each value of n, the wave-front surface itself will locate somewhere along and normal to the direction of that n-vector. Total prevailing wave-front area at each n would be (2n+1).

In the illustration, transition vectors s_n portray as straight lines. Their side length numerical equivalents, called s_{ns} however, can interpret as path length that may meander in any manor. Such meandering while retaining periodicity of overlapping quadrant vectors would bring consecutive radial n-vectors physically closer together then as shown. Here the maximum path length-s_{ns}, as a straight line equals s_{nt}. One reason side-length vectors-s_{ns} can curve at path-lengths, is that they effectively signify tangential extent toward accumulating origin-angle-radians traversed from the apex. No matter what "meandering path direction" of the same full extended length each s_{ns} takes en route, the **apex-origin cumulative radian angle** "swept out" traversing that path between-vector tips will be unchanged from the origin radian angle of each concatenated triangle as drawn within a plane. Each such swept out origin radian angle will always accumulate to $\theta_n = \cos^{-1}[n/(n+1)]$ no matter what meandering route the tangential excursion takes. Extents along s_{ns} deviating into and out of the paper plane would not alter the apex origin angle radians traversed by that identical s_n path-length for "triangles" having "undulating s_n" routes.

Figure 15a shows how origin angles of each concatenated triangle form. Whatever "meandering" might occur in the figure 15b flat concatenated-triangle's contour due to "roundabout" s_{ns} path lengths, the identical number of origin-angle-radians will be traversed. That external contour of the concatenated-triangles could for example be a conic surface (instead of square shaped). On that cone, every s_{ns} path length would, for example, bend around the "circular" conic surface but, so long as n-vectors remains straight, the accrued radian angles cumulated from the origin would be independent of the specific curvature each s_{ns} takes. Another reason side lengths of the wave-front might meander is that no conceptual way emerges to prove that they do not.

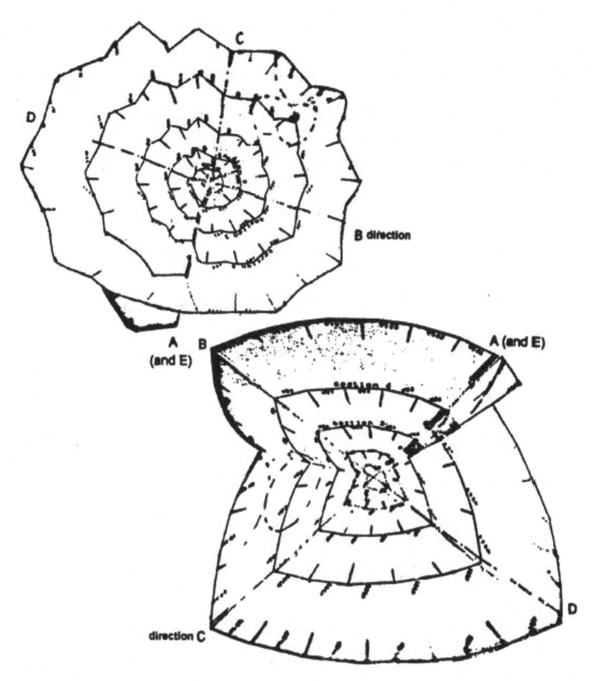

Figure 15 (A) Shows how origin angles of each concatenated triangle form. Whatever "meandering" might occur in (B) flat concatenated-triangle's contour due to "roundabout" sns pathlengths, the identical number of origin-angle-radians will be traversed

The key parameter of relevance will be total-origin-radians swept out by n-vector tips tracking the meandering (or non-meandering) s_{ns} paths per complete cycle around the X-axis. That total remains unchanged howsoever each fixed s_{ns} path-length meanders or how the triangle-planes zigzag. Consistency of accumulated origin—angle-radians irrespective of meandering or zigzagging s_{ns} highlights the fundamental relevance of radians in this Universal Constant for C. It entails 4-cumulative radians per cycle as an **absolute**, exactly one radian per-quadrant. The absolute mathematical definition for one radian coincides with this uniformity directly from natural numbers, as the dispersion of one quadrant of probability wave for (V/C) = 1. Wave-front area during any complete cycle will grow as (2n+1) grows for consecutive n-vector values defining that cycle. For relative motion at exactly light-speed, possibility waves exist that cumulate to precisely 4 absolute radians per repeat cycle or one the absolute radian per quadrant. This was proven by Jim Farned[7]. The 1-radian/quadrant specifies potential wave divergence into the Y and Z directions with progression in that direction-X. For a square shaped wave-front perimeter, solid angle accumulated within every cycle will be one absolute steradian or one radian per side. Harmonic modes having those characteristics are feasible for a spontaneously emitted photon. Since each path length s_n can meander anywhere, constrained only by its allowed maximum length, cyclic conditions also exist where the exterior contour packs into a smaller area then as shown in figure 15. Whatever external shaped contour of concatenated straight-tangential-line triangles can be periodic would also permit a limitless number of additional meandering-tangential-line periodic waves that "flood" the interior of that external-contour state. That is why it cannot be proven that meandering does not occur. Each of those spatial periodic conditions must however satisfy having all quadrant-location n-vectors overlap in there respective-repeat-directions out to $n \rightarrow \infty$. The temporal periods must all be the same and consistent with whenever (2n+1) is a perfect square. Thus, each possible external-shaped-contour of n-vectors described now and subsequently, more generally represents a feasible "wave bundle" that flood's that exterior contour.

Certain equivalences that arise in these analyses are worthwhile to examine. They represent different phenomenological aspects derived from the same set of physical conditions and mathematical assumptions. It has been discussed that in its advance, when wave-front area increases by fixed increments of 2, and the bundle of harmonic waves comprising that wave-front diverge by one steradian of solid angle into the Y and Z directions. This spherical wave-front surface applies for (V/C) = 1 and taken from the apex origin, has a perimeter of exactly 4-radians. For smaller (V/C), perimeter-origin-radians diminish proportionally. The boundary shape of the wave-front might differ from square while still delineating a 4-radian-perimeter/cycle. The square perimeter shape is most easily analyzed.

12) A Logical Origin of Uncertainty & Harmonic Probability Waves

Figure 2 illustrated a concatenated spiral with all consecutive triangles within the single plane of the paper. Nothing articulated herein constrains the right angle bearing direction of each consecutive adjacent triangle of sides n, (n+1), and s_n, to occur within the same plane as the bearing direction of any prior or later triangle planes. **Planes of each concatenated triangle can more generally be at any arbitrary angle with respect to the planes of other triangles.** This allows <u>freedom of bearing-direction</u> (freedom of heading) for each vector-s_n, restricted only as to being at any right angle to its respective n-vector source. See figure 15 for an example.

Moreover s_n can, at least conceptually constitute a "path-length" of total extent $\sqrt{(2n+1)}$ that meanders so that its endpoints may end up separated by anywhere between $\sqrt{(2n+1)}$ and zero. When the endpoints have close to zero separation the tips of all consecutive n-vectors will be the very close together. Origin radians traversed by each (now curving and not in a single plane as for a square surface) apex angle would however be <u>**independent of how or if each associated extent s_n meanders**</u>. With significant meandering of s_n, each "triangle plane comprising origin angle θ_n = arcos $[(n/(n+1)]$" warps into a curved surface, like a section of window drape that pins together to an apex at the top (origin). Radians swept out between every pair of respective consecutive n-vectors from that origin would remain unchanged, independent of the curving path into and out of the paper each s_n might take en route to the next (n+1)-vector tip. Extent of s_n establishes origin-radians-passed-through regardless of how much the side far from the triangle's origin-angle (namely, s_n) meanders out of the triangle plane. The result allows periodic waves formed by n-vectors that surround the X-axis to be comparatively close in (when the ends of s_n are close together), or as separated as straight s_n. When s_n approaches being straight, the periodic wave modes can cover all possible regions of the spherical surface signified by area $A_n = (2n+1)$. Waves formed by n-vectors with meandering s_n will be closest together around the X-axis.

It should be noted that potentially meandering of s_n is conceptual, and these are **spatial periodic waves** characterizing excursions within the Y and Z directions. It might equally well be stated that the tangential extent of all triangles can be of any length up to a maximum of s_n. That description would not demonstrate the accrued radian-origin-angle per total cycle always remaining four absolute radians. Each such possible wave is called a harmonic mode but non-periodic modes are also possible. Most "mode configurations" generated by different triangle directions will be at totally random angles to each other and devoid of inherent periodicity. They could essentially be described statistically by a "random walk" process. Those non-periodic modes prove of negligible interest here. From the enormous array of feasible modes, only a minute few might exhibit cyclic behavior that could result in "possibility" waves. These simulate feasible "paths of least action". Unlimited modes are possible, but non-periodic chaotic ones will not form waves and command lesser attention.

"Vector path-length" s_n defined as orthogonal to n-vector does not constrain which bearing-direction each such right angle (or orthogonal meandering) might occur in. In three dimensions every vector-s_n or it's meander path is not excluded from occurring at any right angle within 360° to its respective associated n-vector. This **unfulfilled degree-of-directional-freedom** in simply **"being orthogonal to a radial vector in any tangential direction" inadvertently injects angular indeterminism into the analysis**. The characterized configuration no longer remains deterministic. All right angle directions remain viable for the direction heading of vector-s_n allowing solutions to emerge depicting a non-specifiable range of "simultaneous" possibilities. Events or circumstances can go each possible way. For that reason, resulting harmonics are called possibility waves and "solutions" materialize as probabilities. All such possibilities have potential to occur "in parallel", although at the termination of the entire process only one "path" will appear to have been traversed. The range of different possible bearing directions provides a mathematical window of opportunity through which only one statistical spatial result occurs. The fact that during analysis an event leads to many possible outcomes within a range of indeterminism does not mean such event and the indeterminism do not have a "cause". A window of indeterminism should be recognized to have a cause just as deterministically definable outcomes attribute to have a cause.

13) Wave-front Dispersion of One Absolute Radian at (V/C) = 1

Objects moving at relative motion (V/C), with a dispersive limit of 1-radian defined from natural numbers by precipitous construction grants a true **absolute Universal Constant**. The 4-radians per full cycle at (V/C) = 1 provides 1-radian/quadrant of angular divergence into Y or Z from the sequence of consecutive integers incrementing (2n+1). Such derivation does not depend upon ad hoc velocity units like distance/time, but only on light-speed C, the maximum rate of motion and dispersion. The result need have very little to do with traditional space/time dimensional units familiar to humans.

The outcome is primarily a consequence of natural number properties. Intrinsic periodicity prevails within mathematical counting-numbers demarcated by whenever the sum of two consecutive integers [as n and (n+1)] is a perfect square. **That perfect-square condition matches an intrinsic physical property of square law space**. The periodicity is exact, as is the intervals between all odd integers. Quadrant partitions within each cycle will also be shown as exact. That is easily demonstrated at large n, in analogue of the exponential definition where n → ∞, but such limit restriction is unnecessary here. **It will be further proven[7] that values of n specifying the four quadrant directions delineating full-cycles via perfect squares of (2n+1) contain no prime numbers from n = 4 upwards to n → ∞**. The quadrants are symmetrical divisors of the number system inextricably corresponding to the distinctiveness of square law space.

It has been cited that relative motion should express using dimensionless denominational units of (V/C) having a numerical maximum of unity and with C ≡ 1. **In this treatise conventional velocity V will never be the reference vehicle of analysis, or used independently as a variable**. **It will always appear normalized by C. Such operation forms a dimensionless fraction F having a range h ≤ (V/C) ≤ 1**. The triangle arm in of extent F and the radian apex angle of possible wave bundles both involve a graphical range where $0 \leq F \leq 1$. It is known that a spontaneously emitted photon propagating at C = 1 can progress through widely spaced apertures in Y and Z as the wave advances along X. A slightly sub-light-speed non-zero rest mass particle can also progress through apertures in Y and Z as a "bundle of possibility waves" that flood an area of the Y and Z directions. However, as (V/C) of that particle diminishes, spacing of the apertures through which it can progress as probability waves diminishes.

14) Interpreting the Wave-front's Tangential Side length s_{ns}

No outward constraint exists to retain any affiliation in the directional-change that occurs between consecutive area-incrementing n-vectors and prior n-vectors. However, for harmonic periodicities to occur imposes some restrictions. A transverse "transition vector" called s_n interconnects the tips of any two consecutive radial n-vectors and it can have any right-angle direction from the originating n-vector. Though called a "vector", the value of s_n, as the calculated orthogonal-transition-extent actually has several alternative meanings. Hereafter they sub-categorize through different nomenclature as s_n s_{nt} for transition extent, s_{ns} for side length extent, and s_{no} for extent from the origin. [The further parameter F also influences transition vector s_n. In section II the different nomenclatures used for representing orthogonal extent $\sqrt{[(n+(n+1)]} = \sqrt{(2n+1)}$ between n and (n+1) will be s_{nF}, s_{ntF}, s_{nsF}, s_{noF}.]

When (V/C) is unity as currently discussed, F equals unity and a less cumbersome description for s_{n1} can be understood in simpler terms as s_n (without the 1). [Later, for (V/C) < 1, the actual-length transition vector s_n may characterize as s_{nF}.] Interpreting transition path lengths between n-vector tips, all s_{nt} vector magnitudes up to that value analytically derived by the Pythagorean Theorem for each right triangle are simultaneously feasible. That will always be an interpretation, and **it leads to a possible bundle of periodic waves within the exterior boundary of the waves being described here in terms of the maximum value of s_n**. Also, waves surrounding any or all n-vector's are possible analogous to the one being described now surrounding the X-axis. The 4-radian exterior perimeter can flood with harmonic-possibility-waves, all having the same periodicity but of smaller excursion into Y and Z than the exterior boundary and of different centroidal directions. "Equivalent" elucidation for these cases has s_{nt} designate as any possible bent or meandering path allowing the analytically derived-extent s_{nt} to curve with the **largest possible separation allowed between n-vector tips** created by the straight-line vector of magnitude s_{nt}. Any starting n-vector can serve as the central axis.

This asserts the largest possible separation value includes smaller achievable values up to that larger limit. The curved or meandering interpretation is actually preferable because only **the total-accrued-origin-radians for the exterior of the bundle of waves is relevant**. That number would be independent of the degree of meandering or which n-vector provides the centroid of which harmonic mode. For now, the X-axis case where (V/C) = 1 is considered, wherein the entire 4-radian exterior-boundary is deluged with the same-periodicity harmonic-waves having differing smaller excursions and central directions. These are all possibilities. Directional indeterminism from the unspecified right-angle directions grant this leeway of interpretation concerning the possibility waves that can result. Because several descriptions for the magnitude and meaning of s_n simultaneously pertain, four metaphors and notations may portray s_n, as a vector, as a path-length, as an extent, and as numerical magnitude s_n. This multi-interpretation derives from all possible right angle directions (paths) being available simultaneously as consequence of uncertainty not definitively restricting which path actually transpires. It may seem abstract and complicated, so for ease of comprehension now, s_n is considered a conventional transverse vector at any right angle to n-vector.

Comprising a segment of spherical surface at some extent from the origin, perimeter of the wave-front area could construct from four "great-circle arcs at right angles to each other creating a "square shape" on that concentric sphere. [Various wave-front exterior shapes are possible, but this shape is treated for its simplicity.] Each side of that square (and any great-circle-arc "parallel" to a side) could have extent s_{ns}, making the wave-front's square area [including the initial unit area], $A_n = s_{ns}^2 = (2n+1)$. The 1 includes and initial unit of area occurring at n = 0. This remains consistent with the method by which area increases by integer-n increments in $A_n = (2n+1)$. In short, integer-n can characterize both: **radial direction, by the rays from n-vector's direction**, and as incrementing integer n, **wave-front surface area normal thereto** (or parallel to the wave-front surface). Therefore, $s_{ns} = \sqrt{(2n+1)}$ calculated at any right angle to n-vector, can respectively represent directions associated with both **the great-circle-arc side-length s_{ns} of** wave-front area), as well as transition extent. In square-law space, it also relates to **the wave-front's radial distance from the origin s_{no}**.

One "justification" for utilizing an orthogonal transition from vector n to (n+1) in incrementing wave-front area is that the square of such transition magnitude automatically equals the prevailing wave-front area. i.e., for transition vector magnitude $s_n = \sqrt{(2n+1)}$ being orthogonal to n-vector and (V/C) = 1, wave-front area associated with integer n equals $A_n = s_{ns}^2 = (2n+1)$. The direction of n-vector will always be normal to the local spherical wave-front area $A_n = (2n+1)$. It is also radial to a "side-length" delineating the great circle arcs of the "square-shaped" perimeter that bounds such area and normal to any local great-circle-arc tangent at n. For a square law description of space, wave-front location from the origin will proportion to the square root of wave-front area. Since each odd integer of s_n corresponds to one cycle, magnitude s_{no} must also associate with the number of prior half-cycles from the n = 0 origin to reach area $A_n = (2n+1)$. [I.e., twice the number of perfect squares between 1 and (2n+1)].

When consecutive bearing directions (headings) of each extent s_n (taken at any right angle to its associated radial n-vector) visualize as all remaining within the same paper plane as illustrated in figure 2, the concatenated sequence of triangles with sides [n, (n+1), and s$_n$,] forms a spiral, initial elements of which appear in figure 1. Each tangential extent s$_n$ equals $\sqrt{(2n+1)}$, so the square of s$_n$ can depict the wave-front's spherical surface area A$_n$ = (2n+1) axially removed from the origin. [For conditions where (V/C) = 1, this proportionality demonstrates as an equality and considered as such for now.] The different possible right angle bearing directions to n-vector are not specified anywhere so any great circle arc within the spherical wave-front area could define the **direction** of a square side-length of that area. Any or all such great circle arcs can feasibly specify possible boundary directions of a "square shaped" wave-front.

This graphical depiction is likely unfamiliar. Radial n-vector increments area A$_n$, an area at right angles to n-vector. This allows s$_n$ inferred at any right angle to n-vector [and one might say unintentionally to area A$_n$ = (2n+1)] **to identify with: both side lengths of wave-front area**, and **the axial extent of the wave-front from the origin**. The **magnitude** of s$_n$ (as s$_{no}$) can numerically signify both a side-length of wave-front area and (as s$_{no}$) its location along axial direction-X. See figure 16.

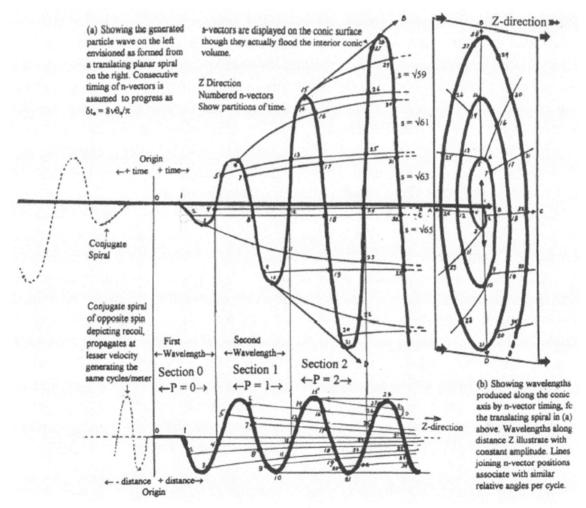

Figure 16 Side-lengths of wave-front area, and the axial extent of the wave-front from the origin.

This feature of multiple associations of vector s_n comprise part of the logic for transitions between n and consecutive (n+1) occurring orthogonal to n-vector. Those right-angle-direction transitions "fit" in magnitude and direction the sizes and position-properties of the wave-front area.

For (V/C) = 1 as currently discussed, wave-front area is considered to comprise from a "square shaped" perimeter contour of great circle arcs, each having exterior side lengths $s_{ns} = \sqrt{(2n+1)}$ on a spherical wave-front surface at radial extent $s_{no} = \sqrt{(2n+1)}$ from the origin. Also, each **<u>magnitude</u>** s_{ns} (as "maximum path-length") could "conceptually bend" along a great circle arc on that spherical surface. That bending would alter the resultant tangential proximity of vector-(n+1) to n-vector, (i.e., the net angle between the two vectors at their final locations). The maximum distance between vector (n+1)'s tip and n-vector's tip would occur with a straight line transition having magnitude s_n, but above and beyond any meandering, shorter distances (treated later in detail for F < 1) as small as almost-zero are possible. For the case of maximum side length distance s_{ns} now discussed (maximum divergence), with each unit-integer increase in n, **wave-front-area** $A_n = (2n+1) = s_{ns}^2$ would increase by exactly 2.

It is noteworthy that any periodic wave modes having repeated overlap of quadrant n-vector's in this configuration would commence at the n = 0 origin and will contain indeterminism from the unspecified bearing direction of each right-angle-vector s_{nt}. Location of the n-vectors that are not at quadrant partitions remained unspecified. Such waves circumvent exponential harmonic shortcomings both by satisfying causality via having a finite origin at n = 0 and by containing indeterminism. Each transition-vector magnitude s_n between any radial n-vector and subsequent radial vector (n+1) will be a function of n [and (n+1)]. The simplest such function is n + (n+1) = (2n+1). That sum can **<u>express wave-front surface area</u>** $A_n \equiv (2n+1)$ undergoing incremental increase by the advancing consecutive integers-n. By more than coincidence, it turns out that for **<u>an orthogonal transition</u>**, straight-line magnitude s_n between the radial vector at n and the next one at vector (n+1) will also be $\sqrt{[(n+1)^2 - n^2]} = \sqrt{(2n+1)} = s_n$. Unknown and unspecified "different possible bearing-directions" of these right angle transition-vectors-s_n introduce indeterminism into the picture.

For (V/C) = 1, transition magnitude $s_n = \sqrt{(2n+1)}$ equates to one "**<u>side length</u>**" of a "square-perimeter" spherical-surface-wave-front-area $A_n \equiv (2n+1) = s_{ns}^2 = [\sqrt{(2n+1)}]^2$. Since surface area increases as a square law of radial distance, magnitude $s_n = \sqrt{A_n} = \sqrt{(2n+1)}$ should also proportion to the **<u>physical location</u>** from the origin of the wave-front itself. Wave-front area proportions to the square of how far it is from the origin. It will be shown, the angular rate-per-radial-distance at which a cumulative "side-length" of wave-front area "spreads out", equals (V/C) [= 1 for a photon.] This makes (V/C) describable in terms of angular dispersion as (side-length)/(radial extent) = radians, or as cyclic extend of excursion in Y and Z per cycle along-X. This describes how and when harmonic wave periodicities can occur amongst the n-vectors (either along X or within Y and Z). Such periodicities constitute viable "possibility waves" associated with relative motion and the propagating wave-front of that motion. Theory reveals how such waves manifest embedded within the wave-front surface area.

15) The Concatenated Spiral Visualized on a Curved Thin Film Surface

This theory hinges on angular periodicity that can arise every 4-origin-radians in location of the n-vectors. Based on rigorous mathematical proofs, the following outlines how this comes about. Whenever consecutive values of $(2n+1)$ is a perfect square and $\sqrt{(2n+1)}$ is an odd integer, the resultant cyclic periodicity emerges within the spiral of figure 17.

For revelation purposes, imagine that spiral drawn on a transparent film sheet. The sheet is then cut inward along each pair of partially broadened radial n-vector lines [the perfect squares of $(2n+1)$] to the origin and tangentially along intervening transition vectors that interconnect those radial lines (figure 18).

This would produce a series of separate "fan-shapes" from the film.

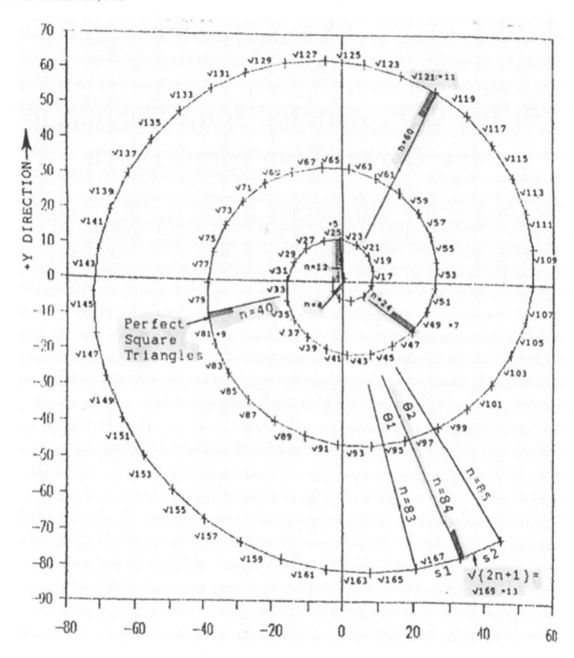

Figure 17 Whenever consecutive values of (2n+1) is a perfect square and √(2n+1) is an odd integer the resultant cyclic periodicity emerges within the spiral.

The spiral is plotted from n = 0 through n = 85. All n-vectors are radial straight lines and tangential s-vectors interconnect them. Perfect square triangles (Pythagorean triplets) are highlighted with shading The two longest triangles exemplify the case with large n and tan θ = θ. Directional components X and Y are presented for reference only.

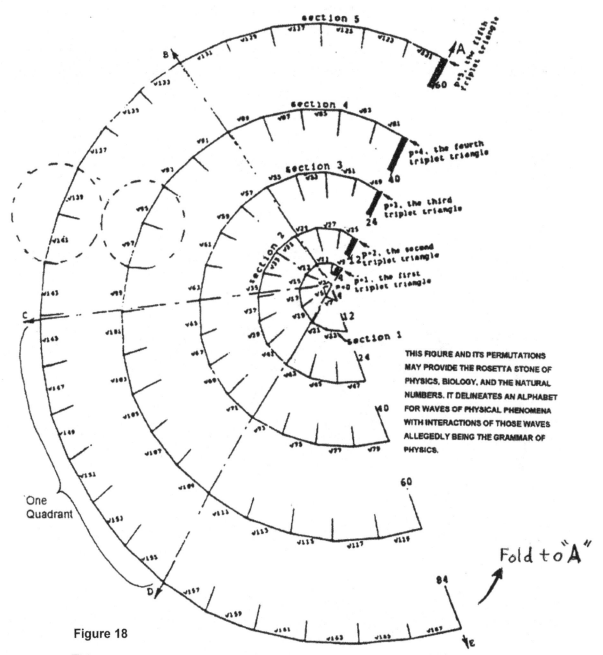

Figure 18

THIS FIGURE AND ITS PERMUTATIONS MAY PROVIDE THE ROSETTA STONE OF PHYSICS, BIOLOGY, AND THE NATURAL NUMBERS. IT DELINEATES AN ALPHABET FOR WAVES OF PHYSICAL PHENOMENA WITH INTERACTIONS OF THOSE WAVES ALLEGEDLY BEING THE GRAMMAR OF PHYSICS.

Fold to "A"

This plot depicts the identical spiral to figure 2 with sections between triplet triangles cut out and those radial vectors replaced in-line at direction A (and E). Radial extents are values of n. Sections comprise from a string of tangential vectors-s_n, each being the square root of a consecutive odd integer, i.e., of $\sqrt{(2n+1)}$. At direction A that square root itself becomes an odd integer, $s_{n@A} = \sqrt{(2n+1)} = 1, 3, 5, 7, 9, ---$. Tangential vectors s_n that straddle direction C approximate even integers out to infinity and at B and D they portray (even+1/2) and (odd+1/2) respectively. Each section occupies $2/\pi$'ths of a complete cycle, or four radians. Were the missing angle of the "fan" between directions A and E cut out, and those cuts joined, each section would delineate a cycle on a cone and there are six such cycles shown to n = 84. The cyclic process continues to indefinitely large n.

81

Figures 19 and 19a illustrate examples of those fan shapes closed to align sequentially at low values of n as the process continues toward $n \to \infty$. For all n values, each of those fans comprises 4-absolute-radians of cumulative-origin-angles. Each separate concatenated triangle's origin angle will be $\theta_n = \cos^{-1}[n/(n+1)]$. Between all consecutive pairs of n-vectors whose values of n form perfect squares in $(2n+1)$, the cumulative intervening respective angles θ_n sum to 4-radians.

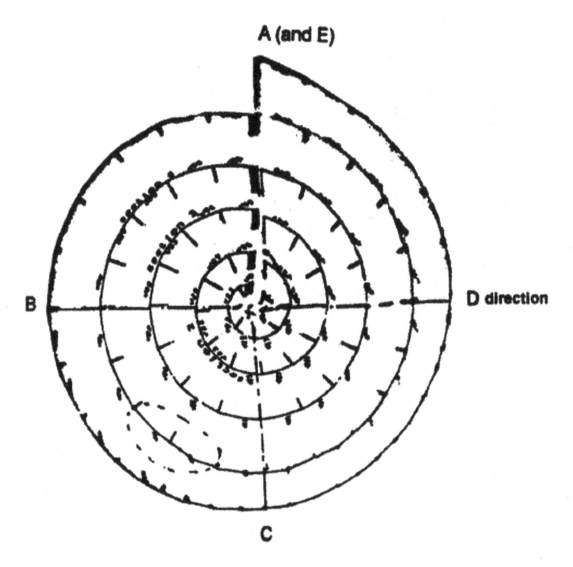

Figure 19 Illustrates examples of those fan shapes closed at low values of n though the process continues toward $n \to \infty$.

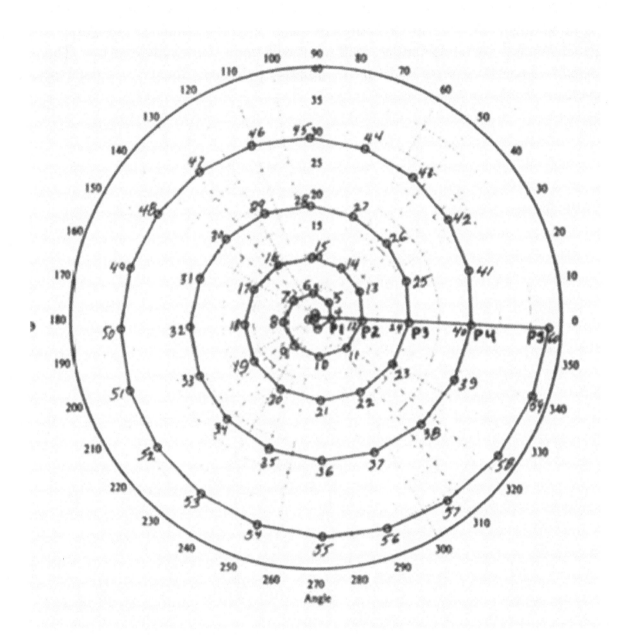

Figure 19A Four radian shift P=5 perfect square alignment forming a cone with the apex out from the page.

Now the planar film distorts into a conic-surface with apex at n = 0, figure 20 that makes possible a 4-radian repetitive cycle "nutating" (re-cycling like a radar dish on target) about the origin between each pair of perfect squares. The four-radian per cycle condition is exact and absolute and during each repeat cycle, three equally spaced partition-directions overlap precisely 1-radian apart in cumulative-origin-angle. Exactness may not be obvious at small n but will simply be asserted for now. Those radial-line-partitions provide definitive **quadrant dividers** for each of the repeat cycles.

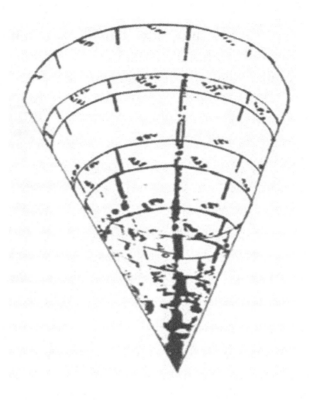

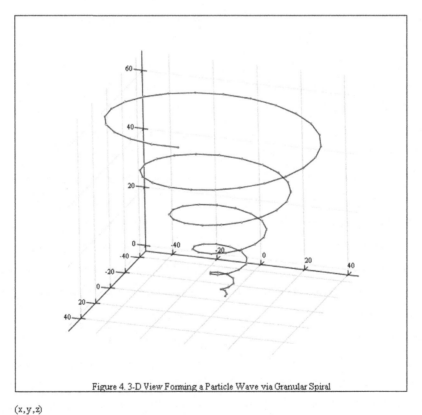

Figure 4. 3-D View Forming a Particle Wave via Granular Spiral

(x,y,z)

Figure 20 The planar film distorts into a conic-surface with apex at n = 0, which makes possible a 4-radian repetitive cycle "nutating" (re-cycling like a radar dish on target) about the origin between each pair of perfect squares.

The figure 21 makes apparent how the quadrant dividers can fall in-line as an intrinsic property of natural numbers. No arbitrary assumptions are invoked in the mathematical conclusion of one absolute radiant per-quadrant or four/cycle.

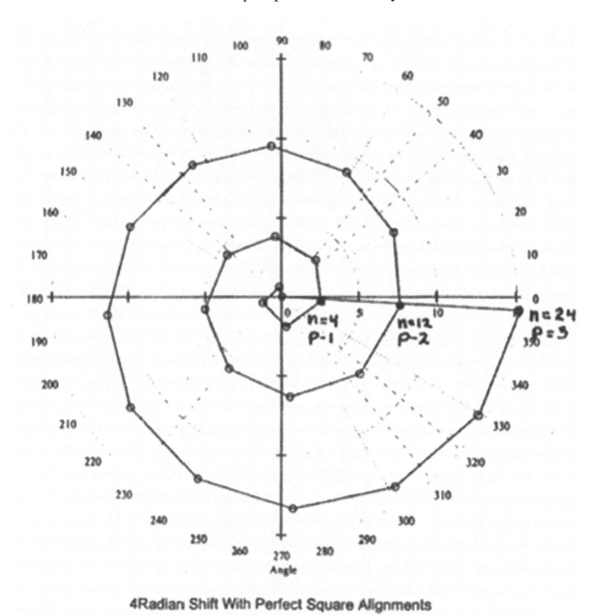

4Radian Shift With Perfect Square Alignments

Figure 21 The quadrant dividers can fall in-line as an intrinsic property of natural numbers

Figures 22, 22A, and 22B elaborate on how the perfect squares delineating total area of (2n+1) may configure periodicity within Y and Z.

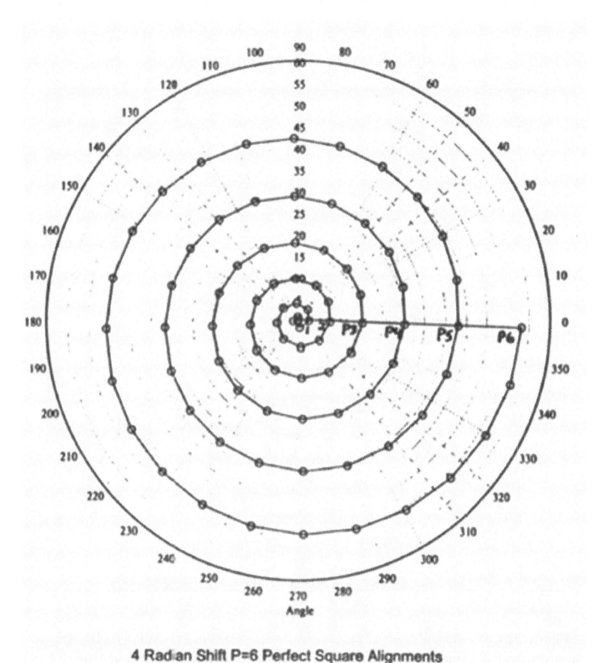

4 Radian Shift P=6 Perfect Square Alignments

Figure 22 One absolute radiant per-quadrant or four/cycle elaborates how the perfect squares delineating total area of (2n+1) may configure periodicity within Y and Z.

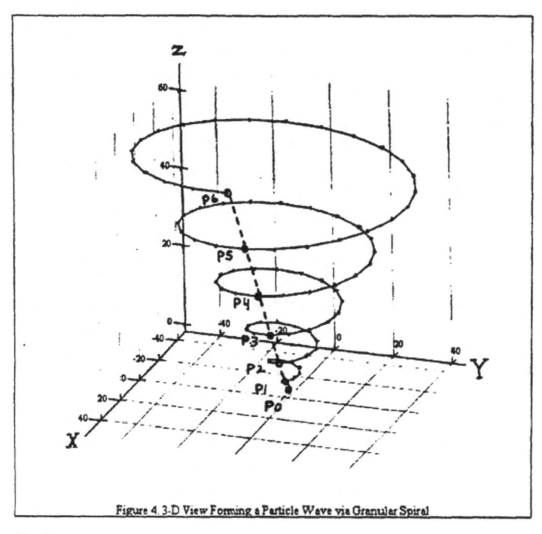

Figure 4. 3-D View Forming a Particle Wave via Granular Spiral

(x,y,z)

Figure 22A (3D view of figure 22) Four radians/cycle (not 2ϖ radians) elaborates how the perfect squares designated as P, line up delineating total area of (2n+1) may configure periodicity within Y and Z

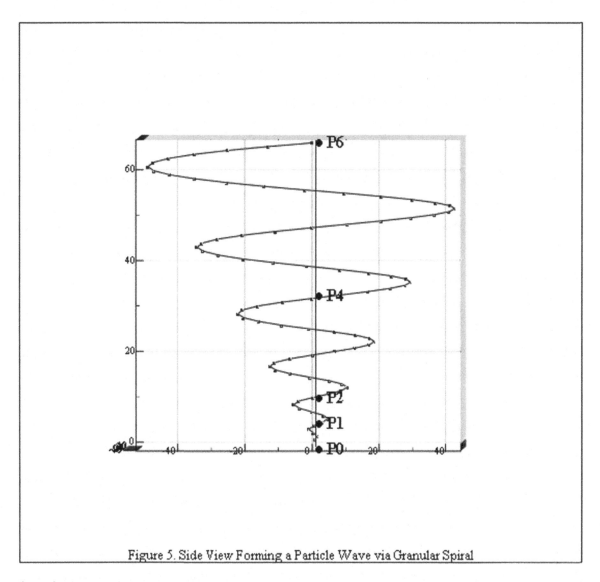

Figure 5. Side View Forming a Particle Wave via Granular Spiral

(x,y,z)

Figure 22B Side view of figure 22A showing waveform structure with four radians/ cycle when perfect squares "P" line up.

To illustrate how n-vector arrays can forms cyclic patterns, imagine all the individual 4-radian-fans superimposed onto one "film sheet" with overlapping n-vectors falling along lines A and B. (See figure 23).

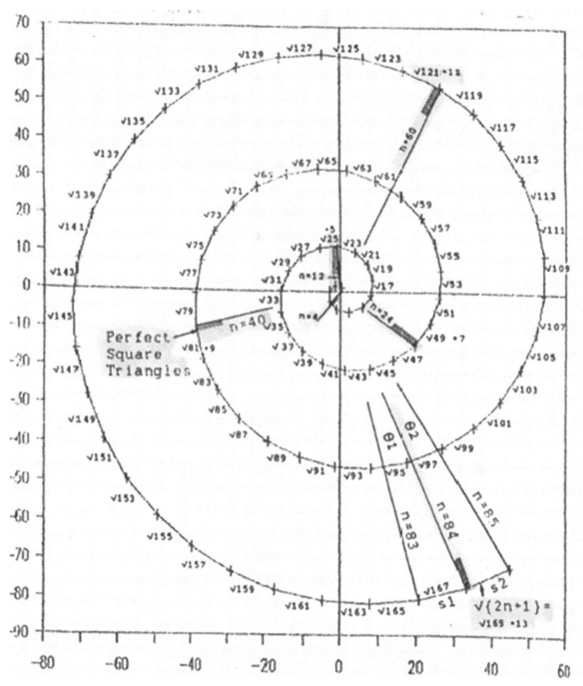

Figure 23 Lines are then cut inward from the exterior to the origin, to form one composite fan-shaped surface, 4-radians wide.

90

Conceptually, those A and B lines are then cut inward from the exterior to the origin, to form one composite fan-shaped surface, 4-radians wide. (Overlook that at very small n the fans might seem to occupy negligibly more than 4-absolute-radians). Joining the cut-out lines A and B together, the film with fans thereupon materialize as a conic surface containing one continuous "spiral" with apex at n = 0. It derives from concatenated triangles that "curve" along each s_n-vector. The radial n-vectors would all remain straight as shown in figure 24.

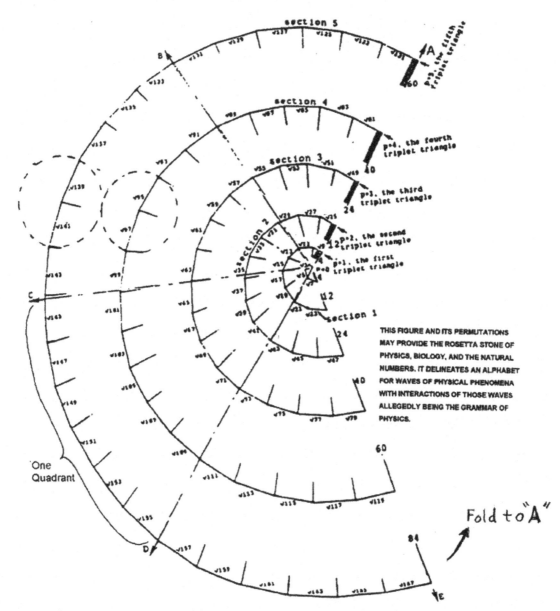

Figure 24 Joining the cut-out lines A and B together, the film with fans thereupon materialize as a conic surface containing one continuous "spiral" with apex at n = 0. It derives from concatenated triangles that "curve" along each sn-vector. The radial n-vectors would all remain straight as shown.

Cumulated origin angle per cycle of nutation between overlapping n-vectors at A and B would remain 4-radians around the conic-surface shown in figure 25.

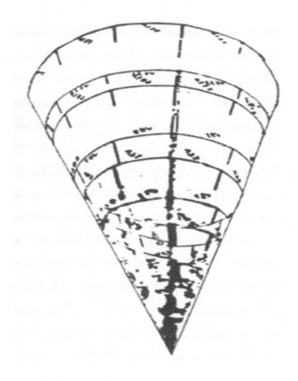

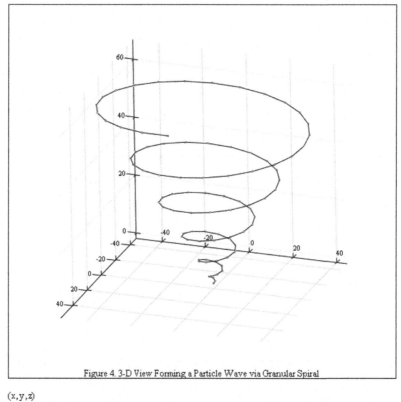

Figure 4. 3-D View Forming a Particle Wave via Granular Spiral

(x,y,z)

Figure 25 Cumulated origin angle per cycle of nutation between overlapping n-vectors at A and B would remain 4-radians around the conic-surface shown.

Figure 26 indicates how the film could alternatively be folded at the quadrant dividers of the cycle into a 4-sided "square tetrahedron" type surface, with each "fan-cycle" summing to the same overall perimeter of 4-origin-radians. Those right angle folds in the film could occur at cyclic quadrant dividers later verified as co-linear, certainly at-large n. [So long as n-vectors remain straight lines the film can be distorted or folded into many different shapes that preserve respective quadrant and cycle directional overlaps.] In discussion for analytic purposes however, either the phrase **conic surface** or **tetrahedron surface** will primarily denote how the fans-on-film bend. More harmonic mode configurations are possible then those two film-surface shapes but they are the simplest to treat.

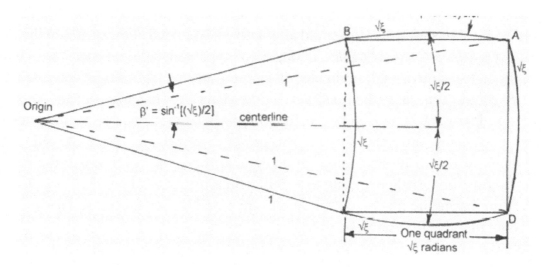

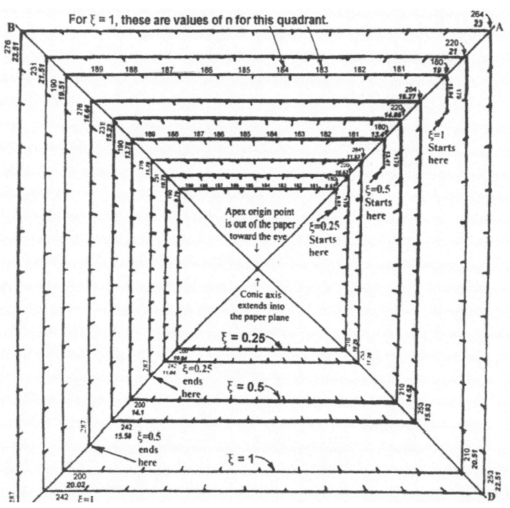

Figure 26 Indicates how the cone could alternatively be folded at the quadrant dividers of the cycle into a 4-sided "square tetrahedron" type surface, with each "fan-cycle" summing to the same overall perimeter of 4-origin-radians.

Each consecutively outward cycle around the spiral demarcated by reaching the originally cut overlapping lines A and B would then entail exactly 4-cumulative-radians of nutation taken about the origin. Whenever wave-front area $A_n = (2n+1) =$ (perfect square), the tangential triangle arms $s_{nt} = \sqrt{(2n+1)}$ on the fans will respectively equal the consecutive odd integers 1, 3, 5, 7, 9, 11, 13,— $= \sqrt{(2n+1)}$—etc. to ∞. These odd integers for s_{nt} correspondingly match circumstances where n = 0, 4, 12, 24, 40, 60, 84,—etc. to $\infty = (4)[1; +2; +3; +4;—+P;$ etc.]. The spacing in n per cycle for each of P consecutive cycles from the origin will be 4P. The spacing per-quadrant will be P, or one additional right triangle per-quadrant manifests in each consecutively outward cycle. If instead of a plane, the original uncut spiral of figure 23 were plotted directly on a conic-surface having a four-radian-from-the-origin-exterior-perimeter, results would be identical to the cut and bent film as described above for visualization.

Various characteristics of this composite fan on film are significant. All radial n-vector lines emerge co-linear wherever the non-integer part of $s_{nt} = \sqrt{(2n+1)}$ is closest to 0 or 0.5, (i. e., whenever $s_n \approx 1, 1.5, 2, 2.5, 3, 3.5, 4, 4.5, 5, 5.5, 6, 6.5, 7$—etc. to ∞). These vector directions represent the 4 separate quadrant-divider partition-lines of each cycle. Those respective radial lines **will always be extremely close to co-linear, and treated as everywhere co-linear hereafter for reasons to be elaborated. They are unquestionably perfectly co-linear as n $\rightarrow \infty$, and very close (if not exact) at small-n. They everywhere exactly overlap in direction for each cycle whenever s_n = odd integer = 1, 3, 5, 7,—etc. to ∞.** Between each pair of odd integer magnitude values when $s_n = \sqrt{(2n+1)} = [1, 3, 5, 7, 9,$—etc.], 3 overlapping co-linear quadrant-partitioning lines exist wherein $s_{nt} = 1.5, 2, 2.5; 3.5, 4, 4.5; 5.5, 6, 6.5;$—etc. to ∞. [For large values of n, all partitioning lines within the every repetitive cycle **exhibit perfect co-linearity with their respective overlap predecessor.**] The three partition lines divide the composite fan into four quadrants per perfect-square-cycle, **each quadrant of <u>precisely 1-origin-radian</u>.** This applies out to n $\rightarrow \infty$, where each 1-radian quadrant can also serve as **<u>absolute mathematical definition for a radian</u>** derived exclusively from the sequence of integers, **<u>independent of</u>** π.

When the fan of figure 24 folds into a conic or tetrahedron surface, the cumulative sum of origin-radian-angles-θ_n (taken once around the contoured conic surface) remains unchanged compared to those angles analyzed on a flat plane,. Though the degree of "curvature" on the cone varies with distance n from the origin, each magnitude (extent) s_{nt} around that tangential curvature retains the same "rounded graphical length" as when s_{nt} remained a straight-line in a single plane. The fan on any curved-surface having straight n-vectors will incur the same 4-radians about the origin per repeat cycle for the summed separate-triangle origin-angles as when the spiral is drawn within a single plane. This would be true for any bending configuration of the thin-film containing the spiral (including a tetrahedron), provided all radial-vectors remain straight in that bending. [That provides another "reason" why magnitude s_{nt} can interpret as any meandering path-length without altering the perimeter origin angles cumulated in that meandering per cycle.] Each such cycle defines exclusively by the cumulative origin angle traversed, established solely through the spacing between odd integers of s_n, **<u>intervals that remain invariant from n = 1 to n = ∞</u>**. Each possible wave with meandering delineates one of many "simultaneously feasible paths" to whatever end result. Potential for meandering expresses the non-deterministic nature of relative motion. These waves present a spatial pattern within the wave-front. If a ballistic (non-accelerated) object comes toward you at close to light-speed, you cannot a priori tell the exact sequence of added area increments in the wave-front that precedes the object.

16) Intrinsic Structure of the Wave's Quadrant Locations

N-vector magnitudes mathematically generate **wave-front area A_n** by accruing integer-n incrementing-amounts in $A_n = (2n+1)$. They also increment **wave-front side length** $s_{ns} = \sqrt{(2n+1)}$, and for-currently-analyzed photons of $(V/C) = 1$, **wave-front extent from the origin is** $s_{no} = \sqrt{(2n+1)}$. With tangential side length s_{ns} and radial distance from the origin s_{no} being the same, radians of divergence per-quadrant characterizing the wave-front will be exactly one radian. **In all three expressions, (area, side length and axial wave-front position along direction X), consecutive integer magnitudes n serve as the incrementing independent variable for wave-front progression.** Virtually by definition, this "independent variable" condition derives as direct consequence of consecutive integers forming a linear sequence. Through integer n, all three "correlate" with each other and with **possible radial-directions of respective n-vectors.**

If any periodicity associates with magnitude n, **it must permeate all three of these parameters and the quadrant positions.** As intrinsic property of natural numbers though, periodicity exists between the odd-integer spacing, 1, 3, 5, 7, 9,—etc. associated with $\sqrt{(2n+1)}$. Therefore, virtually by "**unavoidable design of Nature**", **this analysis indicates harmonic waves and 4-origin radians per cycle can, and most likely due, affiliate with wave-front progression.** Electromagnetic radiation, probability waves, de Broglie waves, and photons, all involve wave-front progression. These processes imply waves of information transfer, matter waves, relative motion, free space radiation, etc. Analysis of their properties constitutes the essence of this theory. **As alternative to harmonic exponentials, they purportedly form basis for all waves directly from natural numbers.** Actual physical waves must diverge at least minutely into Y and Z and must contain indeterminism. For all these processes harmonic roots ingrain within the spacing between consecutive odd integers, 1, 3, 5, 7, 9,—etc. Periodic waves in physical phenomena are thus fundamental to and inextricable from the sequence of ordinal numbers.

The four quadrant dividers indicate why alternative to a cone, the composite fan-shaped-film could equally well fold along lines A and B and those quadrants thereby partitioning the exterior surface into a 4-sided "tetrahedron". The basic topological configuration characterizes a wave on a conic [or tetrahedron] surface **with half-cycles demarcated at integer values of $s_n = \sqrt{(2n+1)}$, and full cycles**

wherever s$_n$ = odd integer[*]. In-between "peak and valley" quadrant positions fall near where s$_n$ has a non-integer part of 0.5. As example, when n increases from 24 to 40, wave-front area A$_n$ = 2n+1 increases from 49 to 81. Between those perfect square values, s$_n$ = √(2n+1) goes from odd number 7 to odd number 9. Therefore, both those n-vectors at n = 24 and n = 40 can be perfectly coaxial in direction when mapped on a 4-radian cone [or tetrahedron], being one complete cycle apart in angle around the conic surface traversed during the intervening values of n from 25 inclusive through 39. Values of n at quadrant positions will be at or closest to 28, 32, and 36. Each consecutive outward cycle, occurring wherever A$_n$ = 2n+1 again becomes a perfect square, can result in co-linear overlapping n-vectors to those at n = 24 and n = 40, etc. This process continues with three intervening quadrant positions from n = 1 until n → ∞.

Every consecutive outward cycle from the origin around the conical fan exhibits one more "compartment [concatenated triangle] per quadrant" then its inward predecessor. Figure 14? makes that apparent. One additional radial n-vector with its associated s$_n$ vector occurs per quadrant, or four per cycle. Therefore, the number of prior outward cycles from the origin (called P) always exactly equals the number of compartments, quadrants, and the number of radial n-vectors per quadrant.

Magnitude values of s$_n$ = √(2n+1) will traverse 4-half-integer increments per full repetitive cycle, and thus **s$_n$ indicates the number of prior half-cycles per integer of its magnitude**. Prior full cycles occur at odd integers of s$_n$ so prior half-cycles correspond to consecutive integer values for s$_n$. Therefore at any s$_n$ magnitude the number of accrued cycles from n = 0 is P = (s$_n$ + 1)/2, or 2P-1 = s$_n$. **Proportional "information" regarding the number of full cycles from the origin and half-cycles from the origin around the cone embed within integer magnitudes of s$_n$, [and s$_{nt}$, s$_{ns}$, and s$_{no}$] with spacing governed by the equal intervals between all odd integers.** As a variable, integers of s$_n$ signify half-cycles of the wave from the origin out to n → ∞.

---

[*] It is noted in passing that the transition location under the F = 1 condition effectively reduces (n+1) by unity. Then the sum of two consecutive values of n would become n + n=2n, rather then (2n+1) for An. There would then be no area increment introduced at n = 0 and all perfect-squares would occur at the even integers. Those even integers are the exact mid-cycle location of the periodicities under analysis. If the leeway of this condition is granted under the prevailing indeterminism, it may be seen how those mid-cycle quadrant positions overlap exactly for all n. The issue of exactness at small n is not worth the analytical complexity of treatment at this point. This does permit another set of harmonics in the wave bundle based on even perfect-squares of 2n. Since cycles can occur in either direction (and can begin at different points) even further harmonic sets are possible.

Even though concatenated triangle-plane-directions can be arbitrary or have s_n bent along a meandering contour, the origin radian angle traversed by each meandering s_n [or by "zigzagging triangles"] would be identical to respective origin-radian-angles for the planar illustrated triangles in figure 2, each such angle being $\theta_n = \cos^{-1}[n/(n+1)]$. Irrespective of whether all or most triangle plane directions are arbitrary [or s_n meanders], co-linear n-vector circumstances can feasibly exist wherever $(2n+1)$ is a perfect square, (i.e. where $s_n = \sqrt{(2n+1)} =$ odd integer). With almost-arbitrary triangle planes all n-vector's having associated-tangential-magnitude-s_{nt} at or closest to an even integer, (as well as where s_{nt} is closest to having a non-integer part of one half), can emerge close to co-linear. Those values of s_{nt} represent possible quadrant dividers for a feasible wave. Toward large n, the "almost" becomes exact. Such conditions depict possibilities, however remote, among the enormous total possibilities allowed by all the different and random-direction triangle-planes and feasibly meandering tangential extents.

Under such circumstances, a periodic wave can also occur where n-vectors are not constrained to a conic or tetrahedron surface. They could be anywhere inside that 4-radian exterior surface **so long as all four quadrant-divider directions overlap cycle to cycle**. Divisor quadrant lines where s_{nt} magnitudes entail half integer increments could then all lie primarily inside the conic surface of the originally disclosed cone, or at least not diverge from each other by more than ± 2-cumulative-radians about the origin. Each possible cycle would still comprise 4 cumulated radians formed from separate discrete-triangle origin-angles, just as in the originally discussed case. This would be equivalent to all the possible ways to put folds or bends into the thin-film conic surface fan while still maintaining straight n-vector's, with four of them per cycle always remaining co-linear in the basic format of figure 20. Examples are shown in figure 15.

On a tetrahedron surface, the spiral rendered here by concatenated vector triangles accrues 4-origin-radians per repeat "cycle". Each quadrant forming a planar side of the tetrahedron partitions every cycle into 4 distinct compartments **of one radian each**. This can convey though the wave-front of a 4-quadrant wave diverging as it progresses along X from an origin. Such waves disburse from axial-direction-X into the two orthogonal tangential-directions, namely into Y and Z. Each specific periodic mode represents one possible circumstance wherein all consecutive n-vector's within each quadrant lie along one planar surface diverging from the X-axis. A conical exterior surface conceptually illustrates by "bending" s_{nt}-vector magnitudes along the "conical exterior surface". However, the right-angle bearing direction of each vector-s_{nt}, in relation to its n-vector, in general need not align along a tetrahedron or conical surface, or even within planes facing directions that relate to prior or subsequent s_n-vectors. Each tangential-going s_n can occur at arbitrary directions relative to each other. This allows the possibility for concatenated triangles to all lie in totally arbitrary unrelated planes, rather than within one single plane, as was employed to form the film that bent into a cone. All accumulated origin angles θ_n per cycle (or per-quadrant) will be identical however, no matter what directions the triangles take. Similarly, the degree of meandering for each s_{nt} extent will also not affect the net origin angle accumulated per cycle.

17) SECTION II

18) Dimensionless F² Along Direction-X As Equal to (V/C)²

The flooded bundle of harmonic waves within one steradian of dispersion from the origin resulted from multiple-possible bearing directions for right-angle transitions from each consecutive n-vector tip to some location on the surface of an origin-concentric-sphere of radius (n+1). All right angle transitions initiate at the smaller radial extent n and terminate at the next higher concentric-spherical-surface at radius (n+1). We now explore what happens if analogous right angle transitions **commence not precisely at integer n** but from **partway between each n and (n+1)**. One might visualize "earlier-or-later-transitions" between n and (n+1) as due to the altered rate of motion, from negligibly small to approaching light-speed, where time at the object appears "bypassed" for the observer with increased (V/C). Then, transitions between n and (n+1) would not onset exclusively from a right-angle specifically at the tip of vector n, which applied for (V/C) = F = 1. At slower motional rates each transition would have additional axial component beyond n along the 0-to-n direction, with subsequent directionally-unrestrained tangential right-angle bearing course from that axial location to (n+1). Such composite transitions having both axial plus right-angle tangential components would then effect a transition at an acute angle to the 0-to-n direction comprised of those axial and tangential components. Resulting transition angle to the n-vector direction might be anywhere between 0° and 90°. Were it 0°, **transition locations from n to (n+1) would lie along the axial direction beginning from n. Were it 90°, the transition would initiate at the tip of n-vector as has been heretofore analyzed for (V/C) = 1.** Figure 5 graphically displays an example of a transition emanating from the 0-to-n direction heading for (n+1) at a location along the 0-to-n direction F^2 less then (n+1). Such diagonal transitions from n-vector would have an axial component of $(1-F^2)$ with a right angle tangential component advancing to (n+1) emanating from a location along the 0-to-n direction at $(n+1-F^2)$. Variable F has significant graphical and physical meaning and will be shown as equivalent to (V/C).

A spiral, as displayed in figure 6 results. The figure provides a graphical rendering of how motional variables interact at different values of F = (V/C). For now, parameter F^2 can have any value $0 \leq F^2 \leq 1$, this exemplary illustration drawn for F^2 of about 0.3 and $(1-F^2) = 0.7$. As Section III elaborates, instead of each transition vector having an oblique-direction extent $s_{nt} = \sqrt{(2n+1)}$, for these circumstances it becomes $s_{ntF^2} =$

$\sqrt{(2nF^2+1)}$. When F^2 is unity, this corresponds to the earlier case where $s_n = \sqrt{(2n+1)}$ and the subscript $_{F^2}$ is then deleted for simplicity. At the other extreme where $F^2 = 0$, each transition extent becomes $s_{nt,F^2=0} = 1$ and all vectors lie along the same co-linear axial-direction line. The spiral would then shrink to a single straight-line as with the advance of a traditional scalar variable. For each circumstance of fixed-F^2, it is mathematically interesting that **the resulting spiral retains periodicities at precisely the same values of n**, **namely wherever (2n+1) is a perfect square**. Quadrant dividers also occur at the earlier discussed n-values. These conditions were proven by Jim Farned[7].

Accordingly, each such spiral drawn on a single plane or film as in figure 22 could have that film bend into a specific conic or tetrahedron surface (or actually any surface maintaining straight n-vector's) with complete cycles periodically reoccurring at the identical values of n. However when $F < 1$, the cone's perimeter-origin-angle at the apex, α_a accumulated for each such repeat cycle become smaller than 4-radians. In fact it becomes $\alpha_a = 4F$ radians for any F value. For F between zero and unity, cumulative apex angle α_a in figure 22 will respectively alter from 4-radians maximum to $\alpha_a = 4F$-radians. Figure 26 shows how fans plotted on a planar film surface having different F^2 values could bend into distinct origin-angle-cones or tetrahedrons. When a "fan-shaped" film, constructed with 4F origin-radians folds at the quadrant dividers into a tetrahedron surface, the cumulative origin-radian-angles-per-quadrant of that tetrahedron will be F radians.

Each fixed value of F allows harmonic waves that can "surround the X-axis with periodicities always occurring at the same integer n values. Similar periodicities can also surround any n-vector with the axial case being discussed as exemplary. All A wave bundle interior to any 4F radians/cycle perimeter (or F radians per side) similarly exists for each value of F. **The smaller F, the narrower will be the apex angle of the encircling cone or tetrahedron of-vectors around the X-axis.** Each concatenated triangle's origin-angle diminishes to $\cos^{-1}[(n+1-F^2)/(n+1)]$. Instead of the solid angle within the conic surface containing 1-steradian [namely 1-radian by 1-radian for F =1], it becomes F^2-steradians [nominally F-radians by F-radians for a "square-shaped wave-front"]. For any value of F, it still remains that the planes in which a triangle containing n and the adjacent (n+1) triangle occur, will differ arbitrarily in direction from other triangle planes. Of the enormous number of triangle-plane and meandering possibilities, multiple sets of 4 unique directions from-the-origin exist for each F where equal-cumulative-angle-quadrant-partitions directionally overlap for every cycle. Within the tetrahedron (or whenever shape exterior) comprising F^2 steradians, exclusive groups-of-four unique-overlapping-co-linear-directions define the quadrant partitions and delineate cycles. Triangle planes might zigzag in any manner inside the outermost tetrahedron (or whatever) exterior. Cyclic periodicities can occur so long as values of n articulating all respective quadrant-divider-directions overlap.

Analogous to the F = (V/C) = 1 case, a bundle of axis-surrounding n-vectors forming harmonic waves is possible. Beyond the specific periodicities on the tetrahedron's surface, waves can flood the interior of each tetrahedron comprising F^2-steradians. That enormous bundle of possibility waves result from meandering s_n and orthogonal transition components of multiple heading-directions. They progress from along the 0-to-n direction to the affiliated spherical surface of radius (n+1) at respective locations $(n+1-F^2_f)$, where F^2_f can be any value between h^2 and 1. From this mechanism, for any $h^2 \leq F^2 \leq 1$, possible-wave-bundles covering an entire spherical wave-front of F^2 steradians manifest from an occurrence at n = 0.

When wave-front area increases by fixed increments of 2 F for each integer-n increase, [as alternative to by 2], the resultant square-shaped wave-front side length diminishes from unity radians to F radians on each side. The wave-front then encompasses a total solid angle of F^2 steradians instead of 1-steradian. Wave-front area diminishes as F^2 as side length diminishes as F. Reduction in wave-front area growth-increments by the factor F bears mathematical equivalence to having orthogonal transition components [during advance from n to associated (n+1)] transit from the n-vector direction at axial position $(n+1-F^2)$, instead of at n. When those inter-integer transition components shift from occurring at [n+0] to occurring at $[n+(1-F^2)]$, the corresponding wave bundle angularly diminishes its exterior boundary, cumulating to a 4F-radian total-origin-angle per cycle, rather than 4-radians/cycle. Periodicities defining each repeat cycle will still occur at the identical values of n however, namely whenever $\sqrt{(2n+1)}$ = odd-integer, independent of the value of F between $h \leq F \leq 1$.

A conclusion of this work is that for (V/C) = 1, cycles along-X define by wherever the (2n+1) term in wave-front area $A_n = (2n+1)$ is a perfect square. This extends to a possible restatement for the square law nature of space. Though for all cases, wave-front cycles from the origin increase in proportion to the perfect squares of $A_n = (2n+1)$, for (V/C) = F < 1, area of the wave-front diminishes as $A_{n,F} = F^2(2n+1)$. A side length of the wave-front becomes $\sqrt{[F^2(2n+1)]} = F\sqrt{(2n+1)}$, and so the cyclic excursions occurring within Y and Z diminish as F compared to when F = 1. While retaining **proportion to a square law increase, <u>parameter F acts as a modifier on the angular extent at which wave-front diverges under that square law</u>**. Also, the faster an object moves relative to an observer, the greater will be the perceived comparative area increments of 2F = 2(V/C) by which its wave-front grows. It is this reduction in area-accruing-rate with diminished F = (V/C) that results in smaller angular spread of the wave bundle as the wave-front expands. For extremely slow-moving everyday objects, the wave-possibility-bundle will be so narrow (i.e., (V/C) radians), the object describes very much like having a Newtonian trajectory with zero angular spreading. The conic-surface then becomes exceedingly close to a cylindrical surface, which would be applicable at F = (V/C) = 0 limits, if that were possible instead of (V/C) → h. The waves described would then closely approach harmonic exponentials and analogous expressions verge on [Y → sin (ωt)] with quadrature [Z → i cos (ωt)], and a wave divergence of zero. That circumstance would constitute "plane waves", with polarization established by the overlap in direction of n-vectors that produce perfect-squares of $(2n+1)$. Thus it is seen that these Unified Waves can encompass and correspond-to traditional sinusoids at one mathematical, albeit non-physical limit condition.

For spontaneously emitted objects, rather then those guided, accelerated, or stimulated, wave-front area identifies the surface location of "possibility waves" where an object moving at (V/C) relative to an observer appears to "exist" (or can exist) in transit instead of exclusively along the X-axis. The possibility waves distinguish those regions occupied by feasible harmonic modes (among the totality of all modes) where uncertainty due to relative motion permits the object to manifest under the circumstances. Each of those modes articulates a "possible course of motion" that the observer could conceivably perceive the object to have taken in the form of a wave. In effect, while un-interrogated, "the object takes or can take all those routes in parallel". Upon final detection, the object will have taken only one of those courses as its actual "apparent trajectory" and that course seemingly will have occurred in the form of the wave that specific harmonic mode represents. An object may appear as a seemingly solid object when "stationary" relative to an observer, but while moving at (V/C) it embraces increasing wavelike properties with increased relative motion. Increased motion associates within an increased window-of-uncertainty. These properties manifest within the wave-front that grows in steradians with $(V/C)^2$. Objects moving at (V/C) manifest as a spread out (divergent) bundle of possibility waves diverging in proportion to (V/C) radians. That spreading stipulates where the object might have gone in its motional course. An object whose relative motion is seemingly negligible, zero, or stationary, will however still diverge at least (V/C) = h-radians. Planck's constant, h-radians depicts the angle formed by the smallest-cycle-of-excursion into Y and Z directions for a full cycle along-X. It is the minimum possible and unavoidable dispersion from direction-X into directions Y and Z.

Accordingly, for all F, $s_n = \sqrt{(2n+1}$ = integer indicates where half-cycles of the wave-front occur and the value of each respective axial n-vector. For $F^2 < 1$, half-cycles still occur for n-values where $(2n+1)$ is a perfect square, but the respective origin radian angle into Y and Z delineating wave-front area will decrease by F. Then each square side-length of the wave-front area must become $[\sqrt{(2n+1)}]F = \sqrt{(2n F^2 + F^2)}$ instead of $\sqrt{(2n+1)}$ when F = 1. Wave-front area still **proportions** to the square of distance from the n = 0 origin, [or the square of wave-front side length when $s_{n(F<1)} = F\sqrt{(2n+1)}$], confirming that wave-front area must then increase in increments of 2 F for each integer increase in n. Thus, axial direction integers of $s_n = \sqrt{(2n+1)}$ specify transpired half-cycles from the origin for any wave-front location. Cycles occur between where s_n = consecutive odd integers and mount up to that integer number P = cycles from the origin. For $F^2 \neq 1$, the "square" side length of the wave-front diminishes to $[F\sqrt{(2n+1)}]$ and its area becomes $A_{nF} = F^2(2n+1)$.

The wave-front emanating from a moving object grows in fixed increments of area. **Indeterminism enters the picture because where, (in which positional direction) each subsequent increment of area gets added within the wave-front is a priori unknown**. From the quasi-infinite number of possible "patterns of area addition", only a very few can lead to spatial periodicity in positioned-consecutive-areas throughout the entire wave-front excursion. Those periodicities depict feasible harmonic modes that can represent the object in transit.

Included indeterminism in an expression means all feasible routes (paths) can be taken or are allowed simultaneously within the window of that indeterminism. Everything constrained within that bounded range of indeterminism is possible. Nothing can be excluded from that margin of uncertainty. Indeterminism in wave-front-information-transfer grows in proportion when fixed added-area-increments become coarser. That coarseness of those fixed area increments gives rise to increased dispersion rate for the advancing wave-front. Dispersion designates a region of inability to know what goes on inside that dispersive solid angle. Dispersion is a manifestation of uncertainty and this theory shows how it (and indeterminism) proportion to the motional rate $(V/C) = F$. Harmonic periodicities occurring within the dispersion angle label viable potentialities for real physical outcomes to emerge. The dispersion rate expressed in radians varies in accord with the degree of motion (V/C), and expressed as solid angle steradians, as $(V/C)^2 = F^2$.

19) Wave Bundle Dispersion from Direction-X into Y & Z

Perfect square conditions with related quadrant dividers assert symmetry within natural numbers. Those quadrants will be shown to provide innate partitioning of all prime numbers in addition to describing the natural makeup of all waves. **Values of n above n = 4 that delineate quadrant directions are never prime numbers**. Such properties of waves, their quadrants and prime numbers, are intrinsic within the sequence of integers-n. It should be noted that "wave-front size" of Unified Waves portrayed here need not designate with an abscissa of time or distance. Those are not the independent variable here. The waves can designate with an abscissa of n, perfect square of (2n+1), or cycles of displacement into Y and Z. Moreover, only quadrant locations of each cycle really enjoy definitive articulation, intervening wave-shapes between quadrants tend to be indeterminate for each periodic mode comprising a wave bundle. Exactly how triangle-planes zigzag or meander between quadrants is unknowable except for certain specific analyzed cases, like on the surface of a tetrahedron. In general each such mode specifies through the overlapping directions of quadrant n-vectors, not by all the possible zigzag trajectories between them.

Figure 9 develops a description of how periodicities can form from wave-front area increments produced by increasing n. Out to $n \rightarrow \infty$, full cycles repeatedly occur at perfect-squares of $A_n = (2n+1)$. The area of each small square will be shown to be F^2, [equaling unity for the initial case discussed where $(V/C) = F = 1$]. Two such increments are added for each consecutive integer-n. Wave-front area increases created by each consecutive integer n will be $2F^2$, [or 2 when $(V/C) = 1 = F^2 = F$]. For any F, composite area of the wave-front at each n amounts to $A_n = F^2(2n+1)$ with wave-front side-length being $s_{ns} = F\sqrt{(2n+1)} = $ [F(odd integer), at the perfect-squares]. In every sketch within the figure 9, the depicted wave-front illustrates as a "projected view" from the origin, or from behind the origin, which designates via the dot in the center of the initial n = 0 area. The small circle at the leading edge of each subsequent pair of area increments articulates a projection of the vector-direction (from the n = 0 center) that each respective n-vector would end up at for a tetrahedron exterior surface. The periodicity inherent to every full cycle thus becomes apparent as well as the quadrant-dividers which all fall in straight lines. At any given n, wave-front location for $(V/C) = 1$ is not at "distance-n" from the origin but at $s_{no} = \sqrt{(2n+1)} = \sqrt{A_n}$ from the origin. Each integer value of s_n along the X-axis represents a half-cycle traversed since, $(s_{no}-1) = 2P$, [e.g., @ n = 4, A_n = 9, s_{no} = 3, P = 1; @ n = 12, A_n = 25, s_{no} = 5, P = 2; etc.].

Offhand, it might seem surprising that the incremental areas represent as square shapes when the composite wave-front interprets as a spherical surface. However, the square root of each incremental area transferred to Y and Z derives precisely from linear extent F^2 along-X "that transition s_{nt} bypasses". The question of whether square areas suffice to depict a magnitude of area in relation to a curved spherical surface is moot for several reasons, including the fact that units of area are never delineated. Namely, if area units are all a micron by a micron, as a square, such area would have virtually identical surface area as a spherical surface defined by great circle arcs of one micron by one micron separation. This analysis takes place at very large values of n because the increments must be of quantum size and not gross squares as depicted in the diagrams for illustration reasons.

The wave-front ahead of or at the object grows in fixed increments of area. Indeterminism enters the picture because where (in which positional direction) each subsequent increment of area becomes added within the wave-front is unknowable. From the quasi-infinite number of possible "patterns-of-area-addition", only a very few can lead to spatial periodicity in area placement that sustains throughout the entire wave-front excursion. Those periodicities depict feasible conditions to represent the object's motion. Since s_n registers half-cycles into Y and Z, increased (V/C) can alter their degree of excursion. The portion $(1-F^2)$ steradians associates with X, with the remaining F^2 portion delineating steradians in Y and Z. The amount of X-axis bypassed (i.e., F^2), being commensurate with the object's relative motion squared "causes" each added area increment to "occur earlier" within the progression, (i. e., closer to the tip of n-vector when approaching light-speed)" becomes "unavailable", bypassed, concerning where insertion of additive area-increments occur. The geometric circumstance depicted by $(1-F^2)$ and (F^2) partitioning describes (i.e., models) that phenomenological process of bypassed space and time for area additions. `

The size of each area increments emerges as the uncomplicated expression $2F^2$ [= $2(V/C)^2$]. This simplicity is understood by considering the case when (V/C) = F = 1 and area increments are 2. Then transitions initiate at the tip of each n-vector and progress orthogonally to (n+1) from the origin. Essentially everything becomes bypassed at light-speed, and a wave-front of one composite zero-thickness spherical-surface all occurs "at once", in terms of what the observer perceives. Wave-front area A_n becomes (2n+1) and for consecutive integer values of n each added area increment of 2 occurs in "zero time". This represents the largest possible added area per transition and matches the greatest transition extent $s_{nt} = \sqrt{(2n+1)}$. That magnitude also depicts all "square sides" s_{ns} of the wave-front area.

It should be noted that nothing **geometrically** prohibits F from becoming greater-than-unity. However, if such circumstance came about, each transition would have to pass through conditions (territory) of smaller n, in the process of reaching larger (n+1) from n. That would correspond to super luminous motion, which is physically unrealizable and thus **limits F (and F^2) to** <u>**unity**</u>. One might conceptually analyze on paper, conditions of super luminous motion by examining the circumstances where F exceeds <u>**unity**</u>. The <u>**unity**</u> limit also manifests as the wave-front dispersion angle for light-speed being exactly <u>**unity-radians per-side**</u> [per quadrant]. The <u>**unity-value**</u> of that <u>**absolute**</u> radian is what establishes light-speed as <u>**unity**</u>. It is the condition where <u>**unity-steradians, (being a 1-radian by 1-radian solid angle of uncertainty**</u>) exists, which dispersion is the result of relative motion (V/C) = <u>**unity**</u>. It is also the condition where the probability of finding the moving object within <u>**unity-absolute**</u> radians is <u>**unity**</u>, and the probability of finding the object within <u>**unity**</u>-absolute-steradians is <u>**unity**</u>. The probability of finding the object entirely within the spherical wave-front is <u>**unity**</u>. When <u>**unity**</u> describes the maximum rate at which information propagates, distance and time from an observer become numerically equal. Only one numerical value associates with light-speed and it is <u>**unity**</u>.

Since wave-front area-additions by increments of 2 constitute the largest area increments per integer of n, applicable for (V/C) = 1 = F, that case must also represent the largest wave-front area $A_n = (2n+1)$. That wave-front area occupies a segment of concentric spherical surface extending into the Y and Z directions. The wave-front and anything associated with a photon, then has zero radial-direction-thickness. It must be a surface everywhere equidistant from the origin. Now consider the circumstance where (V/C) = F < 1. Then s_n transitions initiate from a vector extent of $(1—F^2) = [1-(V/C)^2]$ somewhat greater than n-vector along the zero-to-n-direction. The consequence of occurring "later" along the zero-to-n-direction is that transition-magnitude s_n to reach (2n+1) becomes smaller and added increments of area per integer of n diminish in relation to 2F. But now the "wave-front" might be interpreted as having some "radial-direction thickness", or there exists a component of wave along the X-direction in addition to exclusively traversing the Y and Z directions as existed for F = 1. At the extreme where F approaches zero, periodic wave cycles tend to occur solely along the X-direction, much like any periodic frequency envisioned to propagate in a given direction. The extent of the quantity $(1-F^2)$ along the X-direction would then approach unity. These portray the types of waves we are familiar with, as might occur in a coaxial cable, twin lead, or plane wave. They are typically portrayed as a sine wave along-X, or as a sinusoidal variation in time at any given value of X.

Thus, over the full range of motion covering where (V/C) [= F] is negligently small, to light-speed, periodicity characterizing the motion goes from delineating totally axial cycles along-X with minute excursion into Y and Z, to a partially-axial and large-excursion tangential-periodic-pattern of added area increments in Y and Z. An exclusively-tangential periodic-pattern of area increments occurs in Y and Z for $(V/C) = 1$. This exposes distinctions introduced by relative motion, contrasting a simple proportional change in distance per unit time as traditional velocity specifies.

Relative motion "causes" each next increment of information that can propagate from object to observer to occur at a "closer distance" and "reduced time" because the motion alters the "location" where wave-front-area-additions occur. This manifests as the transitions that produce area increase must occur closer and closer to "earlier vector tip n" as $F^2 [= (V/C)^2]$ increases towards unity. An object moving at light-speed relative to an observer essentially consumes (utilizes) zero of the observer's time because it reaches each foot of closer distance at a time that is one nanosecond earlier to the observer. That is exactly the difference in time for each foot of separation en route. Any information about, or description of the moving object must "coalesce" into one spherically-advancing wave-front surface as depicted herein. Extent along-X cannot materialize for the object with $(V/C) = 1$ because it "passes-through distance-X" in zero of the observer's time". Accordingly, relative motion produces a shift within the information-transfer process, from **being sequential in axial-X and time for negligible motion, to being a tangential periodic pattern comprising wave-front-area-increments within Y and Z at light-speed**.

Mentioned in an earlier section, indicating cycles and energy-time as dimensional equivalents, the smallest cycle-of-excursion in Y and Z transferred from X corresponds to a transferred unit-of-energy-time per cycle along-X. As the cyclic wave progresses along-X, a minute incursion exists in Y and Z directions, the greater (V/C), the greater the incursion and the greater the diffuse angle of uncertainty. The minimum constitutes a minute-digression cycle (or small unit of energy time) occurring in the transverse directions. Even though periodicities have possibility to manifest within, interior of the diffusion region remains indeterminate regarding the structure or course taken within Y and Z. The smallest such incursion depicts Planck's constant, which represents the minimal indeterminate radians of dispersion from any X-direction into transverse directions Y and Z. That is why the expression for photon energy E can be so simple as (energy E propagating along X) = (the minute energy-time per cycle fraction transferred into Y and Z) (presumed cycles per second along X) = $h\nu$. At light-speed, that proportionality portrays the energy exclusively within the zero-thickness spherical-surface-wave-front embracing Y and Z, which characterizes the photon. Saying it in words: (The energy associated with the photon along X) = (the fractional transfer coefficient per cycle h)(the cycles associated with transfer ν) = (the energy within the zero-thickness spherical-wave-front comprising Y and Z). It indicates why h designates as radians, being the ratio of tangential over axial; namely (Y and Z cycles)/(cycles in X), or (energy transferred to Y and Z per-unit of energy in X). The statement can also be made that: **Planck's constant is that fraction of light-speed that quantifies the minimum statistical internal motion of smallest entities comprising all physical things. Each such smallest entity is**

not characterize by a fixed point in space, but occupies an effective region of "motion". It means a so-called idealized-Euclidean-line, more realistically, along its extent of one axial-unit-of-distance, will have diverged one Planck length into Y and Z, [or at the rate of (Planck's constant) radians.

Planck's constant describes that fraction of the speed of light that all particles statistically move at the minimum. That understanding corresponds with the smallest dispersion in an otherwise-presumed Euclidean-line. A line can define only by physical objects (smallest particles or what ever entities), not by imaginary points in conceptual space. Thus, the straightest straight-line will have a dispersion consistent with the minimum motion of the particles that comprise that line. Rather than containing "fictitious points in space" visualized by human mathematicians to form a perfectly linear sequential array of such hypothetical points (as in a Euclidean-line), real points define by actual smallest particles, which must entail some statistical variation in position. This distinction whereby the minimum motion of all particles (things) is not zero but characterized through h radians, might view as the distinction between a Newtonian deterministic-world and the actual world having Planck's constant of background quantum motion everywhere.

For all intents and purposes, particles moving at small (V/C) cannot advance through even pragmatically close-spaced apertures. Such particles become less and less "wavelike" in terms of ability to contain spatial periodicities within information associated with their negligibly small wave-front area. With reduced (V/C), they possess narrower and narrower dispersion angles. Since the wave bundle of particles that might pass through apertures for any given (V/C) should graphically behave similar to the illustrations for graphical variable F as expressed herein, it is not unreasonable to associate (V/C) with F. The graphical picture provides a model for what is happening. The dispersion angle of F-radians graphically decreases in exact proportion to (V/C). That says the wave's axial-extent transfers less and less further into Y and Z with diminished (V/C). The object then becomes less and less likely to progress through apertures in Y and Z with decreased F [or (V/C)]. Or, comparative axial-direction "dimensional extent" perceives to sacrifice with increased (V/C) while transverse-direction dimensions grow.

This work hopes to explicitly demonstrate how h must characterize the limit minimum radians-of-indeterminate-dispersion from X into tangential Y and Z. The transference from X into Y and Z **derives directly from fundamental properties of natural numbers, rather than from a human synthesized model for waves**. It obtains from h being the smallest radians-traversed-from-an-origin. For all F = (V/C), the effective independent variable describes the wave-front area of uncertainty as $A_{n,F}$ = F(2n+1). That area may not portray the historically familiar linear-independent-variable, but it's square root $\sqrt{A_n} = F\sqrt{(2n+1)}$, [a side length of the wave-front] should behave like a traditional linear independent variable. As a cyclic wave progresses along X, a minute diversion of that cycle encroaches into Y and Z directions. The two-dimensional dispersion constitutes a radian angle. It also signifies a minimal unit of energy-time conveyed transverse to X for each cycle along X. The smallest possible ratio of transfer into Y and Z per unit along X represents the radians of Planck's constant. That smallest-transverse-direction cycle surrounding the X-axis invades Y and Z directions during each repetition, i.e., for each periodic cycle when (2n+1) becomes a perfect square in square law space. As such Planck's constant portrays the degree of imperfect-rectilinearity within space; a non-Cartesian quality of space. It denotes the minimum rate of smallest-diffusion-into-uncertainty from a given direction into an orthogonal direction. Such invalidity of Cartesian coordinates becomes even more profound for larger values of relative motion (V/C).

The minute diffusion of h-radians into crosswise Y and Z describes a limit of discern ability below which indeterminacy obscures the precision of any directional course. All feasible Y and Z cycles are "possible", and the object, described in terms of probability waves, takes all those potential routes "in parallel". The two dimensional "width" or dispersive angle of the minimal-window-of-indeterminism allows that potential range even for "stationary" objects. Accordingly, Planck's constant denotes the smallest indeterminate-radians-of-dispersion into directions Y or Z for propagation along direction-X. It corresponds to the [the deterministically unaccounted for, but actual] diffuse spreading of any "idealized Euclidean-straight-line" as that line progresses along direction-X. **Space is not deterministically rectilinear, like built from perfectly square adjoining cubic blocks. Rather, it diffuses into indeterminism with advance along a given direction in accord with the radians of Planck's constant**. That is why the expression for a photon's energy E can simply state as (energy E heading along direction-X) = (the Universal Constant of minimal cross-coupling per cycle from X into Y and Z)(cycles per second surrounding and along direction-X) = $h\nu$. The photon has all of its energy in the Y and Z wave-front, derived from [h], as [(energy)/(cycle per second)], being the minimum transfer coefficient to Y and Z, times the number of transfers (cycles/second) [ν]. At the angular wave-dispersion of 1-radian for a photon with (V/C) = 1, one cross-coupled cycle of that same excursion extent results for each axial-cycle along-X. The cycle along X converts into 1-radian in both Y and Z. That describes the maximum degree of transfer from temporal cycles along X into spatial cycles within Y and Z. At that (V/C) = 1, Energy E heading along direction-X has then all "cross-coupled" into spatial patterns within a zero-thickness spherical-surface in Y and Z. That indicates why "zero dimensional extent" remains along the X-direction as that dimension totally "pancakes" into the Y and Z wave-front at light-speed. A spontaneously emitted photon sustains with zero extent along-X and broad extent across tangential Y and Z as depicted by its wave-front. For very small (V/C), [e.g., stationary objects] that pan caking into Y and Z diminishes to the minimal degree of h^2-steradians as compared to 1-steradian at (V/C) = 1.

The wave bundle's radian dispersion angle into Y and Z also precautions to $\sqrt{F^2}$ = F for right angle transitions between n and (n+1) occurring at (n+1-F^2). Radian dispersion angle F everywhere equals the graphical extent of the inscribed triangle arm. This simply notes equivalence between a physical angle and a graphically portrayed modeling entity: namely between, radian dispersion angle F of the wave-front and inscribed triangle arm F. Along each 0-to-n direction, inter-integer orthogonal transition locations at F^2 less then (n+1) [shown in figure 3, axially along-X at F^2 less then (s_n+1)] correspond to wave-front axial position locating at s_{no} = $F\sqrt{(2n+1)}$ from the origin. Spherical wave-front area would be $[F\sqrt{(2n+1)}]^2 = F^2(2n+1)$. The value of F^2 graphically emerges to portray all resultant features of the mathematical system with [(V/C) and F] equivalent to each other in expressing parameters. As a mathematical truism, they constitute one and the same circumstance for each fixed value of F^2.

Therefore, the graphical extent of inscribed triangle arm F, being numerically the same as radians of wave divergence, will <u>always graphically signify the dispersive radian-apex-angle into Y and Z of the resulting wave bundle</u>. Extent F^2 along the s_n axis analogously designates the solid angle steradians encompassed within Y and Z directions by that wave bundle. Interrelationships within such inscribed triangles of figure 5 provide a graphical picture of wave-front parameters, plus properties of the possible bundle of waves surrounding that axis. Inter-integer inscribed triangle-constructions along the axis graphically illustrate equivalent properties of a diverging harmonic wave. From the diagram sin a = F and sin b = $\sqrt{(1-F^2)}$.

The moving objects treated in this work are primarily spontaneously emitted from a source origin, or ballistically knocked out of a source origin via collision by another particle. Examples would be spontaneously emitted photons, radioactive decay particles, and particles emitted from "billiard ball" type collisions. In this case, it is easy to see that initial motion of the particle having (v/c) = Planck's constant h sets unknown "initial conditions" for motion. By contrast, Newtonian type motion problems are often analyzed where zero initial motion and initial conditions are assumed. The dichotomy between the two treatments is highlighted here because this distinction allows visualization of how indeterminism in direction might increase with increased motion. Actually, all particles (objects) that are not stimulated to emission, accelerated en route, guided by whatever mechanism or tracked in route by reflected photons, etc. are likely equivalent to those in the spontaneously emitted class. This sets up a class of examples that eases explanation, but it does not mean that all moving objects do not require such indeterminism of direction; it is just harder to visualize how indeterminism might come about for the other cases. During the course of motion, the point that those processes might often become is the point of origin for the indeterminism to follow. ***Note:** The above paragraph may belong elsewhere but it was written at this point in my father's manuscript-Lorna Wunderman.*

20) The Relativistic Equation $X'^2 + Y'Z' = 1$ of Contraction & Growth

The question arises, what graphical F might physically symbolize, besides interpretations associated with information transfer occurring earlier (or closer) with increased motion. Certain consequences of F's properties are known from the above stated equivalences. There exists a graphically described parameter F that equals (or can describe) the radian angle of dispersion from the origin into Y and Z for waves progressing along-X. A viable periodic wave of such a bundle of waves could physically advance through apertures within Y and Z and conceptually recombine to interfere beyond. Such interference constitutes a basic property of waves. If F articulated an object's motional rate (V/C) relative to an observer, the faster the object moved the greater the dispersion angle over which it could potentially progress through apertures as a wave. Something moving at light-speed, (i.e., a photon) would entail dispersion of exactly one-absolute-origin-radian into both Y and Z. At close to zero relative motion the object would appear to have no (or negligible) dispersion and could not progress through pragmatic size apertures. [Note: It might conceivably pass through ultra-micro-apertures that are more closely spaced than the motional range of the most elementary particles at absolute zero temperature.]

As a graphical variable, F could provide a link to "perceived" dimensional alterations for objects moving at $F = (V/C)$ relative to an observer. Moreover, referencing figure 5, the inscribed triangle arms geometrically confirm certain simple conservations expressed as $c+d = 1 = (1-F^2)+F^2$, and $a^2+b^2 = 1 = F^2+(1-F^2) = c+d$. Parameter $d = F^2 = a^2$ was previously shown to also equal steradians of dispersion. **These expressions all constitute a zero loss sum to unity**, so that the **variables "share" the maximum radian angle of unity and the maximum steradian solid angle of unity**. Unity is invariably the sum of all probabilities, which then elucidates how one maximum steradian and one maximum radian partition. Since $d\ [= (V/C)^2 = F^2]$ (having a graphical maximum of unity) must dimensionally associate with steradians digressing from X into Y and Z. Then, $c\ [= 1-F^2 = 1-(V/C)^2]$, should correspondingly signify steradians of something. Dimensionally, $b = \sqrt{c} = \sqrt{(1-F^2)} = \sqrt{(1-V^2/C^2)}$ should similarly portray radians because its shared counterpart $a = \sqrt{a^2} = \sqrt{(1-b^2)}$ delineates radians, which are $\sqrt{(\text{steradians})} = \sqrt{d} = \sqrt{F^2} = F$.

If along the scale of s_n, triangle arm-a entails radian incursion into Y and Z (and arm d is steradians diverging from X into Y and Z), then by graphical association, it is reasonable that counterparts b should associate with radians and c respectively with steradians. Just as "size" of the wave-front area associates with expansion into Y and Z with increased (V/C) [= increased arm a = increased F, all respective dimensions along scale s_n should correspondingly relate quantitatively and dimensionally to the physical situation. Increased (V/C) corresponds to [= decreased arm b = decreased $\sqrt{(1-d)}$ = diminishing $\sqrt{[(1-(V/C)^2]}$, which contracts the extent of arm b. These are manifestations of the zero-loss unity-summation for c and for a^2 and b^2. Now Y and Z grow in proportion to F = (V/C) [=a], so this graphical analogy can show how other physical variables alter with a. Assuming the appropriateness of this model and logic, geometry and associated variables indicate that perceived dimensions of an object should modify in X, Y, and Z with relative motion (V/C) in accord with **$\underline{X'^2 + Y'Z' = 1}$**, where X' indicates modified X-direction extent and Y' = (V/C) = Z' = F describes modified side-lengths of wave-front area. This zero-loss sum-to-unity further affiliates waves with probability "of where the object can be found". Here the primes symbolize normalized fractional modification of respective variables as (V/C) varies. For the observer, dimensions in direction-X perceive to contract with increased (V/C) while dimensions in Y and Z would appear to expand, ("pancake outward sideways"). **This relationship provides one simple empirically-testable prediction of this theory.** It grants an unlikely **"conservation of squared dimensional extents"** to unity amongst X, Y, and Z directions associated with relative motion (V/C) along X. Such dimensionality also affiliates with conserved radians and steradians within the probability-wave-bundle.

The figures presented herein articulate but a few of the numerous possible spatial periodic patterns that might exist within the wave-front area. In general, for any given F^2, all values smaller than that F^2 apply to form part of the harmonic wave bundle. Quadrant and full-cycle direction-vectors comprising each set of such periodicities must overlap however, since all periodicities need occur at the same perfect-squares of (2n+1). It is of supplementary interest to note that the issue (of all smaller of n-values then F^2 being allowed) is equivalent to permitting the magnitude (extent) of s_n to meander, so long as in all such cases its cyclic and quadrant end-points fall along the same directions and n-vectors remain straight. This effectively permits all periodicities with "smaller random-walk type steps" then for the maximum step size using F^2, analyzed for clarity.

The question arises as to what "causes" the finite upper limit to information and wave propagation? Findings of this theory infer a self-consistent reason. It has been suggested that Planck's constant represents the minimum radians of dispersion in any direction. That presumably establishes an isotropic diffuse property of space, in contrast to idealized rectilinearity. Instead of a Euclidean line in presumed rectilinear space characterizing any given direction perfectly, every "actual line" (or ray, track, course, etc.) would minutely diffuse with distance by h-radians into transverse directions. There exists a resolution limit, spreading uncertainty, dispersion, or noise level, to Cartesian coordinate rectilinearity and Planck's constant stipulates its value in radians. Under circumstances of physical reality, when an object moves slowly along-X relative to an observer, it traverses distance with a concurrent multiplicity of a priori unknown, but possible ways, it might minutely diverge into Y and Z along its course. That limit-amount, as a minuscule Y-Z excursion/cycle per cycle-along-X represents Planck's constant. The faster the object moves, the greater can be its transverse dispersion. It's Y and Z cyclic excursions then correspondingly advance further and further tangentially. With increased motion, what the observer might retrospectively interpret along-X manifests more and more as possible incursion extents into Y and Z limiting at 1-radian dispersion when F = 1, the object can go no faster. Everything along axial-X has then transferred into orthogonal Y and Z. The maximum rate of motion or that maximum possible degree of divergence constitutes what we call light-speed. Such condition is synonymous with one-absolute-radian and absolute steradian of digression as derived from the mathematics of natural numbers. Nothing can propagate faster because a dispersion angle greater then 1-radian [or F > 1] would have "nothing available" along the X-direction to transfer into Y and Z. This picture illustrates how Planck's constant h, the minimum radians of dispersion, grows to and influences the maximum rate of dispersion, one radian. **The two Universal Constants C and h, thereby limit the degree to which motion can occur. Those constants h and C respectively represent the minimum orthogonal transference between coordinate directions and the maximum orthogonal transference between directions**. It is physically, graphically, and mathematically consistent with why h ≤ (V/C) ≤ 1-radian.

This picture has at least a metaphorical similarity to the pilot waves or quantum potentials proposed by David Bohm[6]. Though the wave-front surface area locates at $s_n = \sqrt{(2n+1)}$ half-cycles from the origin, the tips of all area incrementing n-vectors "extend further away from the origin". Those n-vector-tips will contain precisely the same periodicity and angular information in circling the X-axis as any heuristic modes that prevail within the wave-front surface. Therefore, a mathematical function characterizing surface area A_n via the n-vectors describes some process or effect seemingly "advanced out beyond the wave-front". It might well interpret mathematically like an out-front "pilot wave" that exists and "guides" the wave-front surface to where the moving object might be found. Of course only a mathematical function describing magnitude and direction of surface area prevails at tip locations of the n-vectors, rather then a physical entity. But proportioning to $\sqrt{A_n}$, the wave-front area itself always locates somewhere "along each n-vector", closer to the origin then the function describing n-vector-tips. Accordingly, that mathematical n-vector function, (which plays an important role in the geometric and mathematical formation) analytically appears to be "directing" where the wave-front is or goes. Inherent in the structure characterizing wave-front location and properties will thus reside a mathematical "pilot wave function" at the n-vector-tips seemingly steering the object's trajectory. Even the wave-front is ahead of the object and could mathematically interpret as a leading pilot wave.

The wave-front in space associated with the propagation of possible object locations is not visible. The finite limiting-rate-of-information-transfer through space reveals however, that an "effective wave-front" must always exist associated with information about "happenings" concerning an object. That fundamental and inextricable property establishes how information gets from one place to another, either via photons, gravitons, or whatever field emanates from the interactive event. Relative motion entails no single interactive event, but involves altering situations, information about which can only transfer at light-speed via a wave-front, or consecutive wave-fronts. Here, for simplicity, we only treat one wave-front from one minimal object or one state-of-the-object system. Wave-fronts carrying associated information change must of necessity characterize the state of affairs. Now properties of wave-front propagation constitute a foremost distinctiveness of space and time. The limiting finite speed of light must be direct consequence of how wave-fronts transfer information. Whatever invariants concerning information transfer exist in the isotropic properties of space must vest in rules governing wave-front propagation. Planck's constant is one such isotropic property, and it plays a role at the lowest level of relative motion.

Time and distance are generally interpreted as the linear independent variable (the abscissa) for wave-front advance. In that interpretation, no mechanism emerges for limiting light-speed to a finite value. The information carrying wave-front could advance at any rate and still be consistent with an abscissa demarcated by linear increments of time. When fixed increments of wave-front area become the "linear-independent-variable", its surface area can only grow at some fixed "rate" regardless of the magnitude of that area. That can set a limit. In acquiring information, any observer to events will experience the same process of fixed consecutive area increases in wave-front. Wave-front area must then constrain to only diverge from the origin at a fixed rate affiliated with the "size" of each incremental increase in area, increments of 2 being the maximum. In empirical processes, radian-divergence of the resulting waves broadens in proportion to $F = (V/C)$. Each increment of growth in size is $2F^2 = 2(V/C)^2$.

A limit, established by precipitous construction using the number unity delineates one-radian per-quadrant to the maximum possible rate of radian divergence. At that limit tangential extent equals radial extent and whatever information could have been conveyed along the X-direction "has all transferred to the Y and Z directions". That phenomenon of a 1-radian divergence limit per quadrant **constrains light-speed to its finite value**. Information cannot be "created" and so information along-X plus that within Y and Z sums to a constant of unity. All the information carried by the wave-front ends up within Y and Z at 1-radian of wave divergence where tangential extent = radial extent. Greater information transfer from X to Y and Z cannot occur and that mechanism limits transference to 1-radian of wave-front divergence. That condition converts into the **Standard Universal Constant describing maximum motion** to which all other relative motion rates must compare. That conveys why the maximum (V/C) is 1-radian and why, what we traditionally call the velocity of light C need be unity. Unity radians [(when V/C) ≡ unity] must provide the standard normalizing condition for relative motion. Besides this, there is no way to avoid time numerically equaling distance, which necessitates that they have dimensional units of the same numeric value.

Using the graphical unit-circle's of figure 5 and 6, this theory predicts that for all possible (V/C) motions, a **quantitative description** of the transfer from X-direction into tangential Y and Z directions is given by $\underline{\mathbf{X'^2 + Y'Z' = 1}}$, where X' is the modified fractional extent along-X for any (V/C) and Y' = Z' = (V/C) = F is the modified added extent in tangential directions Y and Z for that respective (V/C). That is, as excursion amounts, the Y times Z product will grow by a degree equaling the dimensional-loss-squared along the X-direction as constrained by a zero-loss unity-summation. This "transfer of dimensionality" from X into Y and Z with increased motion embodies direction-X transferring (via increased diffuse uncertain dispersion) into tangential-excursion-cycles within Y and Z. As was noted earlier, the minutest cycle in Y and Z can also characterize as energy-time, the smallest such unit per cycle transferred being Planck's constant. That is consistent with Planck's constant interpreted as the least quantum of action (the smallest transverse cycle occurring for the minimum (V/C) = h, not zero. One might view Planck's constant h as a minute cycle-of-diffuse-uncertainty directed into Y and Z associated with $(1-h^2)$ cycles out of any particle (object) moving along direction-X. It also indicates the minimum radians of diffuse dispersion along what might otherwise be considered a perfect X-axis or Euclidean-line.

119

21) Periodicities in Random-Walk Growth of Wave-front Area

A wave-front progressing in free space models how information propagates from events within the universe. As outlined herein, radial n-vectors normal to wave-front surface grant an analysis format whereby each element of total surface area $(2n+1)$ correlates in direction with the spherically emanating wave-front. This total area comprises from $(2n+1)$ sub-increments of area whose sequence of spatial grouping can contain periodicities. Every next integer value of n may well deem to effectively designate a subsequent "state of the system" in the compilation process. Such surface areas then characterize by more than a simple scalar value. Each area element confines to an associated direction from the origin, which makes it, as well as total area, a vector. As a vector, consecutive area increments or growth in area can comprise the "independent variable of the configuration". In square-law space those area increments might even be considered "linear independent variable" because space itself grows as the square of axial-direction radius! Feasible harmonic periodicities within 4F perimeter-radians-per-cycle then entail generic information-carriers about the state of the system (perceived in retrospect). Those feasible periodicities result from intrinsic properties within the sequence of natural numbers. No arbitrary model need be involved. In that context, they exemplify properties of waves and carrier particles like photons or gravitons. The wave-front involved must exhibit some degree of divergence as it propagates. While this analysis specifically focuses on relative motion, the concepts and methods can extend to a broader range of the circumstances. Features derived herein introduced by orthogonal advance of transition-vectors having 360 degrees of possible bearing direction can mathematically apply to indeterminism-inclusion-methods in general.

The figures presented here show but a few of the many feasible periodic patterns of area-increment accrual. Such patterns depend upon the varying ways s_n can meander thereby "effectuating shorter steps" taken in the possible random walk additions to wave-front area, while still retaining four-quadrant periodicity. If the moving object has rest mass with $(V/C) < 1$, then each area increment diminishes to $2F = 2(V/C)$, and "spatially closer periodicities" result. Wave-front area then diminishes to $F^2 (2n+1) = (V/C)^2(2n+1)$. The combination of possible periodicities at any $(V/C) = F$ essentially "floods" the wave-front area with potential probability waves. These waves illustrate as "feasible harmonic patterns of the same periodicity" (with synchronous cycles) within the wave-front area. Spatial and temporal periodicities subsist amongst consecutive locations where wave-front area increments grow in sequence. Such periodicities manifest as possible waves that permeate the wave-front. Whenever apertures exist along the field-of-view of the diverging wave bundle, one of the many potential periodicities in that bundle has opportunity to progress through those apertures. As repeat patterns in the sequence and spatial location of incremental additions to wave-front area, they and behave like "standing-waves" in "phase space". Those modes represent possible periodic blueprints where energy or matter that comprises the moving object can be and they may progress through apertures and interfere in route. The modes are perhaps an example of the energy and mass equivalence of waves. Upon ultimate collision or annihilation the one "surviving route" manifests as the "original energy-form or particle". All those propagating "parallel forms" as waves, "delineate potential clones" of the singular particle and only one can endure to materialize. Relative motion facilitates what we consider tangible elements of matter to effectively exist as waves in the course of motion. That property alone distinguishes motion a separate variable from the dimensional ratio of distance and time.

This portrayal of periodicities within the wave-front is consistent with heuristic properties of spontaneously emitted photons. Moving at light-speed C they must have zero extent along the propagation direction and thus need manifest as a "zero-thickness wave-front". That condition must "match" the predictions of any model for entities moving at light-speed. Yet, they can progress through apertures in Y and Z as a periodic wave. That wave-front would **have to embed** a sequential pattern of the relevant periodicities within its surface to cyclically interfere beyond the apertures it goes through. Two essential features are needed to fulfill empirical observations. The wave-front must extend significantly into Y and Z directions and it need contain some embodiment of frequency ν within its surface. With a zero thickness wave-front, there can be "no time available" for cycles/second $=\nu$, so the periodicity embodiment must be spatial. A model that sequentially augments wave-front area with fixed increments resulting in a harmonic manner can satisfy these requirements. Frequency-ν, often envisioned along distance-X, (and time-t) transfers cycle per cycle to "spatial periodicity" ν within the sequential surface pattern of incremented wave-front area.

22) Slowness

There is a novel way think about motional variables that does not alter the presentation here, but yields a somewhat different perspective. If (V/C) provides the appropriate fraction to describe relative motion between the limits of h and the unity standard, why not preferably describe that same situation as a **dimensionless integer based on** the unity speed of light? To visualize the picture from a different vantage, suppose instead of the variable (V/C) for denoting "speed", a "slowness parameter" $S \equiv (C/V)$ were used. Since all entities move relative to one another, why not consider the maximum motion as the base or natural state of conditions and characterize how slow something moves compared to that reference state? Then the slowness variable $S \equiv (C/V)$ would encompass all integers from unity upward to 1/h. Possible merits of the system are primarily conceptual. Nothing needs to be mathematically or algorithmically altered. No fundamental reason exists why rules of physics should be based on every day phenomena as experienced by humans. **We live in a sea of photon flux, all of which continually moves at light-speed, the minimum possible slowness**. Particles moving at light-speed throughout the universe form a very omnipresent sea. Elementary particles in atoms move more slowly. Almost everything else moves slower, a lot slower by up to a factor of 1/h. Why should not the constant-of-slowness based on C be the standard? When macro physical objects considered stationary have energy $E = mC^2$, is it not suspicious from the C^2 that reference conditions of seemingly stationary things entail light-speed C? Most fundamental variables interpret to **increase** in numerical value with deviation from equilibrium as standard. The question becomes what is the equilibrium condition? If it is the photon sea, then the concept of slowness increases in utility. If that constitutes the standard, why view the picture somewhat-narrowly as (V/C) numerically **diminishing** from normal equilibrium?

These viewpoints do not really change any mathematical results, but they force thoughts within a wider horizon. For example, if the upper limit 1/h of (C/V) indicated maximum possible slowness, is that value possibly an integer definable by some characteristic of the number system? Is it perhaps a perfect square and might that be useful to define it in terms of integer numbers? Or does the Planck limit derive strictly from physical characteristics of the universe? Then it might be found to have varied somewhat over the eons of time. If the upper 1/h integer limit established through precipitous construction of the number unity, in analog of how (V/C) references the light-speed a Universal Standard, (as one absolute radian) perhaps all Universal

Constants of Nature could base upon natural numbers. The idea is not ridiculous because nothing really changes by this construal except the concept of what constitutes the standard. It could be constructive to consider light-speed the standard. Though very exploratory, various scenarios can be devised for how 1/h could be an integer of a given category. Although this is a very provisional argument for hypothetical purposes, the concept need not be discounted offhand. It could conceivably provide methodology whereby other Universal Constants might characterize properties of the universe on a meaningful integer basis or powers thereof.

Slowness maximizes during the build up of rest mass. This build up and the associated "stationarity", occurs in sub nuclear particles, within atoms and molecules, in gravitational objects and celestial bodies, within solar systems and in galactic clusters. From each larger scale viewpoint, smaller ensembles tend toward being stationary. The potential utility of slowness as a concept has applicability over the entire range of sizes covering the universe. Over the eons of time, this characteristic has affiliated with forming the physical bodies of the universe, namely with the universe as we know it. The concept of slowness can thus produce unexpected conclusions concerning tendencies of physics. The one absolute radian associated with light-speed based on precipitous construction infers that light-speed has never varied over the eons of time.

All mechanisms involving attractive forces, for example, tend to maximize slowness. These include the strong force, the weak force, force between opposite charges, gravity, etc. Although the consequence of such forces often cause entities to "spin" together locally at a high relative rate, the ensemble of these spinning entities approach "stationarity" from other "stationary" vantages. If the attractive force causes the participating bodies to ultimately collide, the energy of motion generally disperses as thermal kinetic energy, which motion also appears stationary, on average. While attractive forces produce acceleration and relative motion (typically between a pair of bodies), the net effect of those forces is to make the resultant bodies appear "stationary on average" relative to other stationary regions or to other bodies. The forces make the participating bodies act as one larger ensemble (mass) that undergoes less or zero average motion relative to other averaged ensembles. These larger bodies of resultant matter move less relative to other larger bodies of matter (or different regions of larger bodies). Attractive forces thus produce slowness. All attractive forces follow the same tendency and the generalization can be made that overall they produce slowness, seemingly the opposite of motion.

Although this analysis examined the consequences of fixed increments of wave-front area while thus far avoiding a definitive mathematical link between (V/C) and F, other reasons exist why (V/C) and F are equivalent.

23) Conclusion

This book provides insights into mechanisms of wave propagation and presents a theory of the space between integers of the natural number counting system. The analysis presented herein derives circumstances for viably transmitted cyclic modes and the consequence of their existence. Section I addresses the motion of objects like spontaneous emission photons that propagate at the highest rate, light-speed C. Section II covers the relative motion of slower rest mass objects. This treatise does not analyze relative motion in the presence of fields like gravity that could act on the moving object. This thesis purports that our interpretation of relative motion, what we call inertial velocity, is best expressed quite differently than has traditionally been done. This theory shows that the speed of light should numerically be absolute unity, based exclusively on the mechanism by which area accrues on the information-transferring-wave-front generated by events on a moving object. The concepts presented in this book demonstrate that a more general type wave description better satisfies portrayal of a photon's "frequency". The harmonic exponential function "e" is therefore purported to be an inappropriate mathematical function for physically representing propagating waves, photon frequencies, electromagnetic-radiation, and affiliated cyclic phenomena. An appropriate function must involve a reaction that temporally follows an initiating cause and presents a response that includes effects of Planck's constant and indeterminism associated therewith. This theory presents such a function and the waves generated are called unified waves.

The next two sections were crossed out of section I and were to be inserted somewhere in this document but I am not quite sure where they belong. I have added them to the end since I don't feel qualified to determine their appropriate placement in this book-Lorna Wunderman.

24) Assigning "Half-Cycles-From-the-Wave-front's Origin" as $N \equiv s_n$

Along the central direction X-axis at an extent proportional to the square root of area [namely at magnitude $s_n \equiv N = \sqrt{(2n+1)}$] a vector from the origin to the wave-front surface can represent half-cycles, distance, or time. We call the magnitude of that vector $N = s_{no} = s_n = s_{nt} = s_{ns}$, and for $(V/C) = 1$ it has extent $N = \sqrt{}$(area value applicable at n) $= \sqrt{(2n+1)} = s_n = s_{nt} = s_{no} = s_{ns}$. For any specific relative motion at extent given by magnitude s_{no}, partway along and superimposed upon every n-vector direction emanating from the origin lies a conceptual co-directional vector of magnitude $N = s_{no} = s_n$ that could articulate **the physical location of the wave-front along that n-vector.** Namely, a new set of **distance-indicating vectors (rather than area incrementing n-vectors)** could depict where (along the X-direction) the wave-front locates. These new vectors at distance $N = \sqrt{(2n+1)}$ from the origin would all be directionally co-linear (but shorter) then the respective n-vectors they overlap with. Magnitude s_{no} signifies location of the wave-front from the origin and for $(V/C) = 1$, the spherical surface area there would be $A_n = s_{no}^2 = 2n+1$. Symbolically, s_n, was graphically and mathematically derived at right angles to n-vector (which vector magnitude provided the incrementing scale for area A_n), but magnitude $s_n = s_{no} = N$ also has the additional "meanings" of s_{nt}, and s_{ns} in other directions and places. Recollect that the n-vectors were originally devised to increment wave-front-area, so these equivalent magnitudes might be thought of as a "fortuitous property" of the right-angle transition vector s_n.

Magnitude s_n effectively signifies cycles by its odd integers traversed and half-cycles by its integers traversed. If each cycle represented some fixed "wavelength" it would also designate distance the wave-front progressed along the central axis that the n-vector's surround, namely around the X-direction axis. Cycles derived from perfect-squares in $(2n+1)$ constitute periodicities in the wave-front area within square-law space. The square root of that wave-front area must therefore proportion to axial direction. To distinguish between referencing the magnitude of vector s_n interpreted tangential to n-vector, from axially-denoted-half-cycles along the X-axis, the latter axial extent is recognized as the number of half-cycles-N. That numerically represents $N \equiv s_n \equiv$ X-direction half-cycles along the central axis, though s_n's magnitude was established mathematically via a different direction then axial. For $(V/C) = 1$, each consecutive integer N along the X-axis depicts a transpired half-cycle (or wavelength in terms of distance, or time as periods of each cycle), for the possible wave produced by the axis-surrounding n-vectors.

Discussion thus far has shown how wave propagation can analytically derive by having wave-front area increase in **fixed increments** (namely by 2). The accrued number (n) of those 2n-sized increments can serve as **linear independent variable, as well as wave-front area $A_n = (2n+1)$ acting as an independent variable**. In distinction, more conventional circumstances would employ either time or distance as linear independent variable to describe how wave-front advances. In those cases, **wave-front area would vary as the square of time or distance** since the wave progresses in square-law space. The circumstance here also portrays a spatial square law advance because $s_n = \sqrt{(2n+1)}$ equals half-cycles along X or N (also signifying periods or wavelengths) with wave-front area its square as $s_n^2 = N^2 = 2n+1$. In the analysis presented thus far however, consecutive increments of **wave-front area** always remain 2, while in traditional portrayals no such fixed-increment stipulation for wave-front area has been utilized. It is inferred that such fixed-additive-increments to wave-front area result from a fundamental property of Nature concerning wave-front formation. Some rule must govern how the wave-front grows and evidently that describes the rule. **A definitive trait throughout these entire analyses requires that wave-front-area-increases occur in fixed increments (of 2 or less), and the smallest fixed increments can approach (but not equal) zero**. Such a rule for independent variable compels distance and time to become dependent variables for an observer, which we know must take place at large values of relative motion. At smallest fixed increments to be discussed later, wave-front growth in area will become virtually continuous to the point of making the distinction almost moot whether distance, time, or side length of wave-front area, should serve as independent variable.

The waves and wave-front created by invoking integer length vectors along a conic surface that surrounds the X-axis could alternatively describe by **starting the analysis in terms of a sequence of** $N = \sqrt{(2n+1)}$ integer half-cycle along direction-X. Starting analysis by invoking an axial vector N as derived herein, analogous graphics and mathematics would yield the same resultant vector-lengths-n for area incrementing and wave-front location. For the same variables, the picture would be the same irrespective of where analysis began. Side length vectors s_n along a tetrahedron surface would also materialize in the same format as figures 25 to figure 26. No matter what sequence-of-derivations were utilized, or where investigation began, the composite system as described remains mathematically destined to arrive at the same conclusions for the same given conditions. Wave-fronts with periodicities in this sequence of added increments and n-vector's as portrayed with tips spaced $\sqrt{(2n+1)}$ tangential units apart can emerge on a conical or tetrahedron surface. The specific **order** made use of to generate equivalent graphics and mathematics is not germane toward yielding the picture presented.

Since quadrant-divisor lines can lie anywhere **one cumulative radian of** θ_n **angles apart within the four radians/cycle total**, harmonic wave are feasible that completely "flood" the interior of the conic surface, in addition to the cycle formed by n-vector's only lying on the exterior conic surface. Periodic possibility waves might exist anywhere and everywhere within ± 2-origin-radians of excursion in wave-front perimeter. For convenience, they will still be referred to as a wave bundle within a 1-steradian solid angle defined by four "great circle arcs" at right angles on a spherical wave-front $N = s_n = \sqrt{(2n+1)}$ half-cycles from the origin.

25) Analyzing the Unit Diameter Circle between Integers of N

Examination of the integer intervals in N (= s_n) along the central X-axis [or N axis] is warranted. Each such integer interval represents one transpired half-cycle of the prevailing harmonic wave. For reference, an exemplary circle with a diameter of unity is drawn between two arbitrary integers N and (N+1). Figure 5 and 7 depicts a segment of that axis. It is further recognized that F^2 and F are important parameters respectively characterizing steradian and radian dispersion of the resulting bundle of waves. Now to allow graphical evaluation, in each unit-diameter circle at extent F^2 prior to (N+1), a vertical-line is drawn at right angles to the X-axis. At the intersection of that vertical line and the units-circle, another right angle is inscribed within the circle. The result forms an inscribed right triangle in the upper hemi-circle with the arm above axial partition F^2 being F and the arm above axial $(1—F^2)$ being $\sqrt{(1—F^2)}$. This would be true for any value $0 \leq F \leq 1$.

At the center of the unit-diameter-circle, a straight line of length $\sqrt{(3/4)}$ is envisioned coming up out of the paper toward the reader to an origin 0. Then any line drawn from that raised origin point 0 to the circle within the paper plane will be of length $\sqrt{\{[\sqrt{3/4}]^2 + [1/2]^2\}} = 1$. Point 0 can thus be considered the center of unit-sphere that is being cut by the plane of the paper to form the unit-diameter-circle between integers N. Every point on that unity-radius spherical surface will be unity removed from the origin at 0. Any given length-of-line in the paper plane, if it were **<u>redrawn</u>** somewhere curved-onto-the-spherical-surface would numerically register accumulated-incremental-radians-from-the-origin traversed by that curved line. The numerical length of inscribed-arm-a for example, if redrawn curved onto the spherical surface would numerically indicate the cumulative sum of incremental radians traversed from the origin by that length of straight-line-a. It would denote tangential extent along the sphere at one unit from the origin, which signifies radians.

Thus line length-a (and line length-b) both have numerical equivalents of summed incremental radians traversed from the origin. We can numerically register line length-a (and b) as either liner-lengths within the paper plane or accumulated incremental origin radians that would be swept out from the origin if that length-of-line were curved onto the spherical surface. No matter what amount of meandering that redrawn line length-a (or b) took, the origin radians swept out by it would be the same, always numerically equaling line length-a (or b). Therefore, line length-a (and b) numerically

128

designate origin radians equally well to straight-line lengths within the paper plane. It can also be seen why, on the spherical surface, any degree of meandering of such line lengths would not alter the interpretation as numerically-accumulated-origin-radians. Accordingly, setting a = F = (V/C) provides a modeling school for examining how line lengths-a (and b) interact as the origin radians of (V/C) changes, as well as the solid angle steradians = a^2 (=d) changing. We might even overlook the existence of point 0 out of the paper plane and simply register lengths-a (and b) within the paper plane as indicating origin radian, and length-d (and c) registering steradians from the origin. Also, since each space between N and (N+1) [and each unit-diameter-circle] represents a half-cycle, one full-length excursion of arm-a (namely unity) signifies a quarter cycle or quadrant of wave. Hence, line length-a for example, can register as numerically equal to origin-radians-per-quadrant for $0 \leq (V/C) \leq 1$ waves. Four circle-diameters of line length correspond to the 4-radians per complete cycle between each adjacent pair of perfect-squares in (2n+1).

Howsoever cumulative triangle planes interior to that steradian zigzag, each "square wave-front exterior side length" would comprise angles θ_n summing to 1-radian per quadrant. That constitutes possibility for a "flooded" 1-steradian solid-angle-bundle of waves having each orthogonal side diverge one radian from the origin. Independent of the sequence in which this analysis developed, possible harmonic solutions for the originally discussed n-vector array or wave-front entails a bundle of waves progressing along-X and defusing 1-radian into Y and 1-radian into Z. Inherent indeterminism of the system stems from any or all of the waves, (and random modes) within this entire bundle being possible. The uncertainty can be viewed as do to every s_n-path-length having an unspecified bearing direction for its respective right-angle to n-vector. An alternative, but likely equivalent viewpoint would be: there is unpredictability in where a ballistic object approaching you will cross a plane orthogonal to the motion. Such unpredictability increases with (V/C) = F. A conceptual vector N specifying wave-front location along-X can signify half-cycles at integers of $s_n = N$. The wave-front surface itself would intersect the direction of each n-vector "part way along its extent" at $s_n = N$ half-cycles from the origin. Each such radial n-vector direction will always be at right angles to the spherical wave-front area and therefore indicative, in both magnitude (s_n) and radial direction, with where the wave-front surface area propagating away from the origin should be. It is worth remembering however, that n-vector magnitudes do not indicate distance or half-cycles. They constitute an area-incrementing method, though their radial-direction will be everywhere locally-normal to the wave-front surface.

The circumstance would be as shown in figure 1 where wave-front area along each n-vector direction always locates partway [namely amount $s_n = \sqrt{(2n+1)}$] along the radial direction of every n-vector. For any specific n_a, direction of the wave-front's central region will locate at extent $N_a = s_{na} = \sqrt{(2n_a+1)}$ along the central axis. That direction and location characterizes advance from the origin of the propagating wave-front (and the probability waves involved). The spherically curved wave-front area always locates at extent $N_a = \sqrt{(2n_a+1)}$ half-cycles along each n-vector direction, where N interprets in terms of integers matching the odd and even integers of s_n.

Harmonic results herein are primarily a consequence of natural number properties. An intrinsic periodicity prevails within the natural number sequence demarcated by whenever the sum of two consecutive integers [as n and (n+1)] is a perfect square. This periodicity is exact, and quadrant locations within each cycle also become perfect at large n in analogue of the exponential definition where n → ∞. **It will be further proven that values of n specifying the four quadrants for all cycles delineated by perfect squares of (2n+1) <u>contain no prime numbers from n = 4 upwards to n →</u> ∞.**

26) REFERENCES

1 Henley, William: *A Book of Verses* (3rd Edition). New York: Scribner & Welford.

2 I. Wunderman (2000). *"What is a Photon? A Unified-Wave Theory Explained."* Wyndham Hall Press, Bristol, Indiana.

3 I. Wunderman (2004). *"Planck's Constant and Pi. A Unified Wave Theory for Particles and Bioforms."* 1st Books, Bloomington, Indiana

*4 parenthetical note

4 Stoney, G. On the Physical Unite of Nature, Phil. Mag. *11*, 381-391, 1881

5 Planck, "Uber das Gesetz der Energieveteilung im Normalspectrum", Ann Physic 4, 553 (1901).

6Bohm, David "A New Theory of Mind and Matter." PHILOSOPHICAL PSYCHOLOGY, VOL. 3, NO. 2, 1990, pp. 271-286.

7 Farned, James completed a proof but we were not able to locate it. He can be contacted at Jfarned@rain.org.

End Notes

Dr. Irwin Wunderman introduces a new mathematics that greatly simplifies waveform calculations (eliminating use of π, e, i, ∞) and gives unification to fundamental constants and conservation laws with new insights into the integration of Planck time/length within wave, and quantum mechanics. This work is a significant breakthrough in the mathematical treatment of the wave mechanics used in many fields of science.

The use of a 4-radian **granular wave** resulting from harmonic relationship in ordinal numbers is as significant as Leibniz and Newton's application, notation invention and the crystallizing of infinitesimals used in their creation of the modern calculus. During Newton's seminal years of 1666 to 1676, the Renaissance, algebra was resumed from near eastern sources, and geometry from the Greek. Scholars of the time became familiar with classical mathematics. When the new calculus was born, the new ideas spread quickly through the intellectual circles of Europe. Our history shows the importance of the diffusion of these mathematical ideas, and their effects upon the subsequent development of the sciences and technology. Dr. Wunderman with this book, the last of three books on the subject, has just planted such a seed.

Dr. Wunderman's books will be of much value in providing mathematical insights, a greater understanding and valuable new tools used in uncovering the secrets of our physical world.

I have had the good fortune to be a witness to a genius at work. Irwin has been my dearest friend. I had the privilege and honor of providing a sounding board for his ideas and new insight to a different perspective of the physical and mathematical world. This work is the culmination of his vision, his dream, his life's work.

Allen J. Amaro
Fellow Retired Scientist, SRI International

IRWIN WUNDERMAN
(scientist and inventor)

The author produced 16 patents and 25 papers, some attaining international awards. He published two other related books: *What Is A Photon?: A unified-wave theory explained* (2000) and *Planck's Constant and Pi, a unified wave theory for particles and bioforms* (2003). This third book culminates over 40 years of independent research to establish how and why ordinary natural numbers and mathematical relationships express fundamental physical laws through waves.

Work on this theory began in graduate school as the author studied towards his 1964 Ph.D. in solid-state physics, optical electronics, and instrumentation at Stanford University. His early career included solid-state research and development at Lockheed and then at Hewlett-Packard. Nicknamed "Mr. Transistor," he was deeply involved in instrument design, including those for measuring wave frequency, electrical conductivity, and light. He later led HP's first computer division, which produced their first calculator. Thorough the 1960's, his work included development of the first opto-couplers and fiber-optic communication links.

Upon leaving HP in 1967, the author started Cintra, a company that initially developed a line of digital, optical instruments for measuring photons. It later produced a compatible computer/calculator (the Cintra Scientist model 909), which received the '1970 Industrial Research 100 Award' for creating the first scientific computer-calculator to employ algebraic notation and having a data bus permitting real-time integration between digital instruments, keyboards, computers, and network systems. That data-bus became the prototype for the IEEE-488 bus standard, and the calculator, the basis of Texas Instruments scientific calculators. Later in life, the author was on the board of a number of Silicon Valley start ups, including Cetus Corp. He invented bio-medical probes for instruments to screen human tissue for cancer. Despite all these immediately practical endeavors, throughout his career, he also worked tirelessly toward developing a unified wave theory.